HOPE WINS

*A Collection of Inspiring
Stories for Young Readers*

HOPE WINS

A Collection of Inspiring Stories for Young Readers

Tom Angleberger · James Bird

Max Brallier · Julie Buxbaum · Pablo Cartaya

J. C. Cervantes · Soman Chainani

Matt de la Peña · Stuart Gibbs

Adam Gidwitz · Karina Yan Glaser

Veera Hiranandani · Hena Khan

Gordon Korman · Janae Marks

Sarah Mlynowski · Rex Ogle

James Ponti · Pam Muñoz Ryan

Ronald L. Smith

Christina Soontornvat

R. L. Stine

with cover art by **Vashti Harrison**

PHILOMEL

EDITED BY ROSE BROCK

PHILOMEL BOOKS
An imprint of Penguin Random House LLC, New York

First published in the United States of America by Philomel Books,
an imprint of Penguin Random House LLC, 2022
First paperback edition published 2023

Library of Congress Control Number: 2022937040

Printed in the United States of America

ISBN 9780593463956

1st Printing

LSCH

Edited by Jill Santopolo
Design by Ellice M. Lee
Text set in Bell MT Pro

For my beautiful family.
My joy and hope come from you.

CONTENTS

INTRODUCTION

Dear Reader,

In 2018, I published a book called *Hope Nation*, sort of an older sibling of the book you are reading, because I wanted to share stories of hope with the teens in my life who were struggling. Since then, I've been lucky enough to visit with young people who have read stories from that collection, and I have gotten to hear about how those stories have helped them through hard times and made them feel a little less alone.

In 2020, the world as we had known it changed. COVID-19 changed the landscape of how we live, look, go to school, and interact with others. The daily reminder of how our own lives can be turned upside down made me realize why it's so important to hang on to hope. It's not always an easy thing to do—sometimes, it feels downright impossible—but the thing I know is that difficult times in life come and go; with those experiences, we grow as people. The key is to find ways to motivate and inspire our spirits—stories of hope can do that.

In this collection, I've asked some of my very favorite writers and friends to share a true story from their own personal lives. I hope hearing them share their own stories of challenges they've faced in life will help you find your own voice. Each of us has a story that's worth sharing and celebrating.

It's also worth noting that, like choosing hope, we can choose to do good, and for that reason, *Hope Wins* is a charitable endeavor. My contributors committed to creating this book with me as a means to support the North Texas Teen Book Festival (NTTBF), an annual book festival that serves thousands of young readers each year. For their willingness to dig into their memory chests and share with everyone, I thank them all and am forever grateful.

For me, making a decision to choose hope is grounded in the love and support I receive from my family and friends, especially my daughters, Madeleine and Olivia, and my husband, Michael. Thanks to each of you for joining me on this journey. It's not always an easy path, but it's one worth taking. Remember that no matter what happens, hope wins.

Dr. Rose Brock
Grapevine, Texas
2022

EVERYTHING I NEED TO KNOW I LEARNED IN A THAI RESTAURANT

by Christina Soontornvat

This is not a knock to any of my teachers, but the most important things I've learned weren't taught to me in a classroom. They were taught to me in a restaurant dining room (and the kitchen and the cashier's station).

When I was three years old, my parents opened a restaurant in the small town of Weatherford, Texas—the first Asian restaurant in the whole county. My dad, an immigrant from Thailand, saw it as an incredible business opportunity. He was right: loyal customers kept our little family restaurant open for nearly forty years.

When I was a kid, I never gave much thought to what it meant to grow up in that environment—it was just my everyday life. If you had asked me then what the best part of spending so much time at the restaurant was, I would have said it was the endless flow of fountain drinks and free spring rolls.

But now I realize that I learned some big, important lessons about people and about life. And now—like a crispy, hot spring roll passed from fryer to plate—I pass these lessons on to you.

. . .

THE WAY TO A PERSON'S HEART IS THROUGH THEIR TUMMY

Our busiest shift of the week was Sunday lunch. Almost the whole town of Weatherford went to church on Sunday mornings, and then they would show up at our door as soon as the services were over. We'd often have a line that stretched out onto the sidewalk!

Most of the people who lived in our town attended Christian churches. And then they came to eat food prepared for them by people who were mostly Buddhists. When we first opened, we called ourselves a "Chinese restaurant" because at that time (in 1983), people there weren't familiar with Thai food. Over the years, we gradually introduced more and more Thai cuisine to the menu. And we also introduced more and more people to Thailand and our culture. Some of our customers even took trips to visit Thailand. Sometimes they met up with our family who lived over there! So many connections were made between Thailand and Texas: two places that are on opposite sides of the globe from each other. And it all started with food.

Food is simple and primal. It is unifying. I wish people in this world had more chances to share food with each other. How can you be angry when you're chowing down on a dish of garlic chicken? How can you judge someone when you're sharing a plate of dumplings with them?

I'm not going to say something silly, like the solution to world peace is to have political leaders take their meetings at family restaurants. But maybe it wouldn't hurt? Maybe they would pass better laws if they also passed each other the shrimp fried rice? And maybe they would also realize that everyone, everywhere deserves to eat good, wholesome food in a safe place. Maybe they would realize that it's not so hard to take care of each other.

Food is love. Food is peace.

And if you don't believe me, let's eat some mango and sticky rice together. You'll come around.

GIVE THE DUCKS THEIR DUE

Mmm, duck. Tender, with a crispy skin, and drizzled in a sweet, spicy sauce . . .

Sorry. Where was I?

There is a well-known metaphor that says a good restaurant is like a swimming duck: on the surface everything looks calm and smooth, but underneath, the duck is furiously paddling its little feet to keep moving across the water. This was a pretty accurate description of our restaurant. When customers came in, we wanted them to feel like they could leave their troubles at the door and let us take care of them. Their table would be clean when they sat down. The food would be hot and tasty. Their iced tea glass would be refilled before they could even ask.

Serenity. Air-conditioning. Smooth instrumental pop hits playing on the stereo.

Back in the kitchen, it was a whole other story: crowded, hot, and noisy!

Cooks slinging sizzling food in the woks, rice cookers filling the room with jasmine-scented steam, waiters shouting that they needed that order of pad ka-prao five minutes ago!

"Two century noodles, one with chicken! One with no bean sprouts!"

"Where's table nine's appetizers?"

Staff in the back stuffing wontons, crates of dirty dishes being washed, and the clean ones being carted back out to the dining room. Go, go, go!

Seeing what happened behind the scenes was one thing I loved most about growing up in the restaurant. It was like knowing a secret no one else did.

And it showed me that there are so many things in life we take for granted when they go smoothly: our schools, our homes, the businesses we frequent. But there is no one who works harder than the people whose work we take for granted. I try to give those people grace and gratitude because I know that underneath it all, their feet are probably paddling like heck.

KEEP CALM AND RESTAURANT ON

As a little girl, my one restaurant dream was to work the cash register. Our cash register was gray, as big as a microwave, and had these brightly colored buttons that made the most satisfying *clack* when you pressed them.

When I turned twelve, my parents decided that I had finally earned the right to ring up customers. On the big day, I proudly pulled up a stool, put on a big smile, and uttered my first "How was the meal, folks?" as I punched the buttons: *clackety, clack, clack*.

One woman came up to pay with a credit card. No problem, I had been trained on this procedure. But as I was ringing in her amount, I must have gotten a little too carried away with the clacking, because instead of charging her $50, I charged her *$5,000*.

Sweat beaded at my temples, and I imagined this woman screaming at me and making a scene. I didn't really understand financial matters, so I thought that *I* would have to pay for that $4,950 mistake out of my own allowance!

I smiled at her and said, "Will you excuse me one moment, ma'am? I just need to get an extra roll of receipt paper from the back."

Be a duck, be a duck, be a duck, I thought as I hurried to the kitchen and told my mom what I did. She came out and was able to miraculously issue the woman a refund without much fuss. I thought my mom would be so mad at me and revoke my cash register privileges. Instead, she was proud that I hadn't freaked out but had solved the problem quickly and calmly. I felt proud, too. That day, I had earned my duck feet.

YOU CAN'T JUDGE A HUMAN BY THEIR HANDBAG

In the service industry, sometimes you hear people say, "The customer is always right," but actually, sometimes the customer is extremely in the wrong.

One afternoon, my mom was ringing up customers as they paid their bills. *Clackety, clack, clack.*

Mom greeted the next customer in line: an elegantly dressed middle-aged woman. The woman set her large designer handbag on the counter to free her perfectly manicured hands so she could sign her check. She accidentally bumped her handbag with her elbow, and it tipped over, spilling out multiple sets of our cutlery: knives, spoons, and forks (no chopsticks).

Mom stood there, blinking, trying to figure out a polite way to say, *Um, excuse me, ma'am, but are you STEALING OUR SILVERWARE in your four-hundred-dollar purse?*

The woman blinked back at her a couple of times, finished paying for lunch, gathered up her bag, and left without a word. She left the silverware, but she did not leave a tip. Which brings me to a related lesson:

YOU CAN'T JUDGE A BRO BY THEIR BOOTS

We had this one longtime customer: a great big man who owned a small ranch where he raised horses. He always wore scuffed-up cowboy boots, and he always took his cowboy hat off when he came in to eat. He was a quiet man, a country man, and a real polite person. He was one of our favorites.

Well, one day we heard some wild news: that guy had won the lottery! No kidding, overnight he had gone from humble ranchman to multimillionaire. I wondered how he would be spending his money. A big, fancy mansion? Or a fast sports car? Would he still come in to eat, or would he be served caviar by his butler from now on?

The next weekend, he wore the same scuffed-up cowboy boots, the same cowboy hat. He ordered the exact same thing and sat at the same table. He was still the same quiet, polite person. The only difference was that when he was finished with his meal, he left a hundred-dollar bill on the table as a tip.

I figured that this guy probably knew what it felt like to be a duck and how much work it takes. He could have spent his money on anything in the world, but he chose to use it to show gratitude for people's hard work. I always thought that was real classy.

WHEN THEY GO LOW, WE GO, "HI, WOULD YOU LIKE A TABLE OR BOOTH?"

For the most part, the people who came to eat with us were class acts, and the restaurant was a place of mutual respect and kindness. But not everyone in our town was so kind.

Growing up as one of the only Asian American kids in my school wasn't easy. Even though I made some of my best memories and strongest friendships in Weatherford, I also dealt with racism and xenophobia. I got told to go back to China numerous times, was called a "China doll," and was told that "my people" eat dogs.

Sometimes kids would pull the corners of their eyes at me and shout, "Ching chong, bing bong!" Racism is so hurtful and cruel, and it also sounds so, so stupid. Really? *Ching chong, bing bong*? Yeah, you are really proving your superiority with that one, folks.

Anyway, there was a boy who was one year older than me in school, and he was the worst. He would say these stupid, awful things on a consistent basis. But the boy's family were regular customers at our restaurant. They were kind of quiet, not overly warm and friendly but not rude, either. (That kid definitely never let a racist word slip out while he was scarfing down our scrumptious chicken satay.)

My dad and I never spoke about racism when I was young. I worried he wouldn't understand or that it would make him feel bad for moving our family to a town where we were outsiders. But one day I finally decided to tell my dad about this boy. I told him all the mean things the boy said and that surely he was learning this stuff from his parents.

My dad nodded. "Yeah, honey, I know. I believe you."

It was this moment of mutual understanding, where I knew we were on the same page.

So I was hoping that this kid was going to get his comeuppance in some way. I didn't think my dad was going to cause a scene and throw the family out, but couldn't he at least tell the cooks to hide some chiles in his pad thai? Serve him the brown crusty rice scraped from the bottom of the pot?

Instead, the next time that boy's family came in to eat, my dad was just as polite as ever. As far as I could tell, they were served their meal with the same good service as always. I watched them clean their plates, pay, and leave with satisfied sighs.

For a girl who had imagined her archnemesis sprinting for the bathroom with his mouth and intestines on fire from an epic Thai chile—burn, it was pretty disappointing.

It wasn't until later that I realized my dad knew what he was doing. By giving that family quality service and delicious food, he was elevating himself above their ugliness. Now, don't get me wrong, if they had been violent or disruptive, they would have been kicked out. Otherwise, he was going to give them a meal they would be talking about for weeks.

My dad was an immigrant, born poor, who raised himself from a factory job to open a restaurant that people drove a hundred miles to eat at. There was pride in what he could do. There was dignity in being excellent when others expected him to fail.

The harsh truth is that plenty of terrible people never get their comeuppance or see the error of their ways. But they can't take away our dignity. They can't deny our excellence. And we belong here just as much as anyone else.

And if they can't handle that, then no satay for them. Their loss.

WE ARE ALL INFLUENCERS

There is this term in social media right now: *influencer.* By the time this book goes to print, it will probably have changed, and those people will be called *statusticians* or *beezers* or *oozebers* or something. But the concept will be the same: they are the people with millions of followers who are so popular and influential that they can set global trends.

I didn't realize it until recently, but our restaurant was full of influencers. One of the biggest influencers of all was our manager and headwaiter, my uncle Donis. Donis didn't have any social media accounts. He didn't own anything fashionable. He didn't jet to glamorous places. In fact, he rarely ever left Weatherford because he usually had to work.

When my uncle passed away this year after battling cancer, we received stacks and stacks of letters from customers and hundreds more heartwarming messages sent via the restaurant. Many of them said similar things:

"Donis always made us feel so welcome."

"He remembered our favorite dishes and had them ready for us."

"He treated us like we were family."

As I read through these messages, it hit me how much a small act of kindness can mean to someone. Too many people in this world feel forgotten or unimportant. Too many people don't feel like they deserve to be loved. Taking the time to learn someone's name or what they like to eat, or just greeting them warmly and looking them in the eye—you never know when that is going to make a real difference in someone's day. Talk about a superpower.

I wish my uncle had known how powerful he was, how much of an influence he had on all these people. Maybe he did know, and maybe he was trying to teach everyone that they have this superpower, too.

We are all influencers. We all have the power to be good to the people in our everyday lives—the people who matter the most. Out of all the lessons I learned in the restaurant, that one is my favorite.

That, and how to pick out the right dipping sauce for grilled chicken.

Now, who's hungry?

CHRISTINA SOONTORNVAT is the award-winning author of over a dozen books for children of all ages, including the beloved Diary of an Ice Princess chapter book series. Her recent works include the middle grade fantasy

A Wish in the Dark, which was named a 2021 Newbery Honor Book and was chosen as Best Book of the Year by *The Washington Post* and *School Library Journal*, and *All Thirteen: The Incredible Cave Rescue of the Thai Boys' Soccer Team*, which has received numerous nonfiction awards and was also named a 2021 Newbery Honor Book. Christina lives in Austin, Texas, with her husband, two young daughters, and two old cats.

THE COOLNESS EQUATION

by Adam Gidwitz

My whole life, I've wanted the other kids to like me.

Obviously. We all want friends, right?

But when I say, "I wanted the other kids to like me," I don't mean that I wanted *friends*. I mean that there were certain kids whose friendship I *craved*. Like the way you look at a sheet of brownies with peanut butter chips and you're like, *Oh my gosh, I want that so much I'm going to steal the whole pan and hide in my room and shove all the brownies into my face.* (Do you ever feel this way? Or do I just have a weird brownie obsession?) Anyway, there were certain kids who I wanted as my friends *so bad.*

It started early.

I remember feeling this way in the first grade. There was a girl named Jenny who was, through preschool and kindergarten, my best friend. And then Meghan showed up.

Meghan. My blood boils just *thinking* about her.

Suddenly, Meghan and Jenny were hanging out all the time, and I felt *super* left out and *unreasonably angry.* I can still feel those emotions in my chest, right now. I remember one day it got so bad that I swiped a box of thumbtacks from the teacher's desk. And as Meghan and Jenny sat beside each other on the rug, listening to the lesson, I took the thumbtacks, one by one, and I *threw* them at Meghan.

None of them hit her, because I was in the first grade and thumbtacks are terrible projectiles.

But I *wanted* them to hit her. A *lot.*

This feeling is jealousy, and we all feel it sometimes. But the feeling transformed as I got older.

When I was in the third grade, there was a boy in my class named Evan. I thought Evan was *cool. Cool* became an important word in my life, probably starting right then. Evan didn't have the most friends. He wasn't the best at sports. But he was the funniest kid in our class. He also gave off the impression that he didn't really need any of us—maybe because he had two older sisters, who he could hang out with at home.

So he was funny, and independent of us, and he didn't really seem to care what we thought. Without ever realizing it, I came to associate this combination with the word *cool.* I think it became for me an unconscious definition: *funny + independent + impervious = cool.*

Starting in third grade, I *coveted* friendship with cool kids like Evan. Like a tray of warm brownies with melty peanut butter chips inside. I *wanted.*

And in third grade, I got! I actually managed to be friends with Evan. We created a little comedy routine together. We called it "The Bouncing Baby Blues Brothers." We would sit next to each other and bounce against each other and sing: "We're the Bouncing Baby Blues Brothers / All we want is our mothers / WAHHH! WAHHH!" Over and over. And the other kids thought it was hilarious. Oh, how I loved it.

But I wasn't *cool*, like Evan, even though I was a Bouncing Baby Blues Brother. I knew it, and everyone knew it. I might have been funny, sometimes. But I wasn't independent—because I so clearly *wanted* to be friends with Evan. And I certainly wasn't impervious— because if ever someone insulted me, I'd feel really upset. You know, like everyone else. Everyone else, that is, except the *cool* kids. According to my math, they never did.

Over the next few years, the cool boys in my grade started identifying each other and hanging out together. There were four of them.

(Disclaimer: If you asked someone else in my grade who the cool kids were, they may well have named *totally different* kids as cool. These four weren't good at sports—so they weren't the jocks—and they didn't have the largest friend group—so they weren't the most popular. But in my mind, they were the *coolest*. They had *funny* + *independent* + *impervious* = *cool* down cold. And there is *some* objective truth to their coolness, I think. It wasn't all in my head. Because after high school, two of them started a rock band and became kinda famous, and they were on a couple of TV shows playing rock music. Which, by many definitions, is *cool*.)

Well, you can imagine how I felt about this group of cool kids. I *desperately, so badly, painfully, achingly* wanted to be their friend. And you might be thinking, "Why? What's so great about being *cool*?"

I have *no clue*. But I did know that they were truly funny—when I sat at the lunch table with them, they could make me laugh so hard milk came out of my nose.

So they might have been truly cool, but they definitely weren't truly *kind*. A group of us boys would try to hang out with these four cool kids, and they would regularly call us "followers." "Don't be such a follower!" they would say. And whoever they said it to would feel shame—while the rest of the followers would laugh and feel secretly relieved that it wasn't their day to be shamed. Or the cool boys would "ditch" a follower—they'd propose a game of hide-and-seek tag (like hide-and-seek but faster and more dangerous) in the hallways during lunch or after school. When we all were hiding, the cool kids would secretly organize everyone to "ditch" one of the followers, so he'd keep hiding and have no idea that everyone else was gone.

I remember one day, I was successfully hanging out with the cool kids—and feeling really good about it—when one of them said to me, "You remember that time? With that guy? Wasn't that so funny?"

And I, desperately wanting to be a part of this cool group, eagerly said, "Yeah!"

And the cool kid said, "That guy, with that thing?"

"Yes!" I said, laughing along. "Oh my gosh, that was hilarious!"

And then the cool kid suddenly stopped laughing and said, "What are you talking about?" And I felt like an *idiot*, because clearly there was no "guy" with a "thing." And all the boys laughed at how eagerly I had gone along with whatever the cool kid had said. What a follower I was.

Being a follower was the opposite of being independent. And I certainly wasn't impervious to what other kids said about me—when they teased me, it hurt, and everyone could see it. I might have still been funny on occasion, but even that was ebbing away. Because it's hard to be funny when you're constantly worried about saying the right thing or the wrong thing. Trying really hard to be funny is a bad way to be funny.

So I was spending more and more time around the cool kids, and I was getting further and further away from being cool.

One thing that the cool kids had in common was that they liked to skateboard. They weren't amazing at it or anything, but they all did it, and they wore skateboarding shirts and shoes and wallets with chains on them (wallets with chains were, apparently, a skater thing).

I will never forget one trip to the mall, in seventh grade, with my mom. We were looking for clothes for me to wear. And we saw a brand of skater T-shirts that the cool kids often wore. Since I thought the kids were cool, I thought the shirts were, too. Since we were looking for clothes for me anyway, my mom agreed to buy me one.

I wore this shirt to school a few days later. In science class, all the kids had gotten there before the teacher. And one of the cool kids—his name was Chris—looked at me and said, "Why are you wearing that shirt?"

I said, "I don't know. I like it?"

"That's a skater shirt. You're not a skater."

I didn't know what to say.

I knew I wasn't a skater. In fact, I didn't know what I was.

But Chris did. He said, "Poseur."

Which was a word I hadn't heard before. I figured out pretty quickly that it meant "someone who pretends they're something they're not." I also figured out pretty quickly that it was the *opposite* of being cool.

Somehow, through some magic I still do not understand, Chris got the *entire class* to point at me and chant, "Poseur! Poseur! Poseur!" over and over and over again. It must have ended somehow, sometime, because I am not still surrounded by chanting seventh graders. I imagine the teacher probably came in eventually. But I don't remember it ending. In my head, it never did.

I continued to subject myself to the cool kids' teasing, to their invitations to hang out and then be ditched. I wanted to be their friend *so, so badly.* More than I wanted to eat those brownies. A lot more.

Until eighth grade. By then, I had given up. It was too painful. My adolescent heart just couldn't take it anymore. I started hanging out with some other kids—and this was maybe worse than the *cool* kids, because these kids were into bad stuff, and I got into it as well. And then we all got caught, and I stopped hanging out with them, too.

Just before ninth grade began, I made a decision. I decided that I couldn't be trusted to make friends. Either I was gonna subject myself to cruel, torturous teasing or I would get myself arrested. So I decided that—starting in ninth grade—I would have no friends.

And I didn't. Sometimes I sat by myself at lunch. Other times I sat with whoever was around. From time to time I even found myself at the table with Chris and the other cool kids—but I didn't care about them anymore. If they made me laugh, fine. But when we all stood up to take our trays to the trash cans, I made sure to leave the cafeteria alone. And if ever they, or anyone else, asked me if I wanted to hang out after school or come over to their house, I would always half smile and say, "No thanks."

That might sound sad to you. And it did, in fact, feel a little melancholy. But that year, something really strange started to happen. I realized—for the first time in my *life*—that I kinda liked school and was good at it. History class was all about interesting stories from history! Who knew? English class was just a teacher giving you a good book and telling you to read it, and enjoy it, and explain why you enjoyed it. Uh . . . sure! In science, we looked at freaky little monsters under a microscope. That's awesome, actually.

I started to discover what I *actually liked.* Not what I thought would make the "cool" kids like me. What *I* liked. And I did those things. I often did them *well*. And I felt *proud* of myself. For the first time in my life.

I was independent.

Also, I didn't care if the cool kids said something mean about me anymore. Since I didn't care, and also I wasn't trying to hang around with them, they pretty much stopped saying mean things about me. Or, if they said them, I wasn't around to hear them. It created a virtuous cycle. All because I didn't care what they said. So I had become impervious, too.

One day after school, near the end of the year, some boys from my grade were hanging out. I'd never really tried to get to know these guys—they weren't cool, and they weren't popular. But we started chatting, and it turned out they liked a lot of the same things that I did—we geeked out over cool stories from history class, in fact. We started to hang out in the hallways after school more often. And then I was invited over to one of their houses—and I went. We stayed up all night playing a nerdy World War II simulation board game. It was one of the best nights of my life.

Oh, and we made each other laugh. A lot. They were funny. And I was funny.

And also independent.

And impervious.

So was I, according to my own equation . . . cool?

Maybe? I don't know.

But I do know that those boys I played board games with are *still* my best friends today, twenty-five years later. I created a book series with one of them. The other one is my daughter's godfather.

Ninth grade—the year I spent without friends—might have

been the most important year of my life. Because whether I became "cool" or not, I did learn how to be independent. And impervious.

When I was twenty-five years old, I decided to quit my first job to try to write a novel. It was not easy. I needed the strength to abandon my colleagues. I needed the strength to ignore everyone who doubted that I could become a published author. I needed the strength to be alone, every day, working on a book that no one had read or would read for a year. Once someone finally did read it, I needed the strength to hear their criticism—"I'd recommend starting again from scratch"—and not crumble. To keep going.

To be an author, you *must* be independent and impervious. Or close to it.

I don't thank the "cool" kids for being mean to me. They don't get credit for what happened.

I thank my ninth-grade self for finding the strength, somehow, to be alone, and find what I genuinely liked, and allow some true friends to find me.

I don't know how a fourteen-year-old decided to do that—except that I was reacting to an enormous amount of pain.

My response to that pain made me who I am.

And I don't care what you say: now I think I'm actually pretty cool.

ADAM GIDWITZ spent most of his childhood playing with action figures and imagining that he was the greatest basketball player ever. Now he writes books like the scary fairy tale *A Tale Dark & Grimm*, the Unicorn Rescue Society series, and the only Newbery Honor winner ever to feature a dragon with deadly farts, *The Inquisitor's Tale*. *A Tale Dark & Grimm* is now an animated series on Netflix.

THIS CAN'T BE HAPPENING TO GORDON KORMAN

by Gordon Korman

"*. . . and so, starting tomorrow, everyone's going to write a novel.*"

The word landed with a resounding *thump* in our seventh-grade English class, like construction workers outside had dropped something really heavy—a telephone pole or a three-ton block of granite. Heads swiveled around on necks, creating an interlocking network of anxious glances around the room. A novel? *Us?* We were twelve. A couple of us had turned thirteen. And this guy expected us to write a *book?*

Our eyes eventually returned to Mr. Hamilton at the front of the classroom, searching for the mischievous grin, the crossed fingers, or the "April Fools!" that would tell us this was a joke. (No such luck. It was February.)

The teacher went on to explain how the project was going to work. We would have a forty-five-minute class period each day to write. An outline was due the first week and a chapter a week after that. By the end of the year, we'd each have completed a short novel. Easy-peasy.

"He's delusional!" my friend Mark complained. "He ran one mile too many and scrambled his brains!"

19

This take was less far-fetched than it may sound. Mr. Hamilton wasn't a real English teacher. He was the track-and-field coach. Thanks to teacher cutbacks and a couple of maternity leaves, he turned out to be the only warm body free to cover our class during that period.

Mr. Hamilton was in training for the Olympics as a distance runner. Practicing consisted of running to and from school—thirteen miles each way—every day. So it wasn't beyond the realm of possibility that the miles and the long, cold Toronto winter had gotten to him somewhere between his front porch and room 124.

I was already formulating a plan. As an only child, I was pretty skilled at making stuff up. That was how I kept myself entertained with no other kids around. I made up games. I made up stories. In my twelve years, I'd given my imagination more exercise than Mr. Hamilton had given the legs that were going to propel him to Olympic glory.

By the time I got home, I knew exactly what my novel was going to be. Back then, my two favorite movies were *Airport*—about a plane crash—and *Jaws*—which had terrified me all last summer. So I was going to write about an airliner that crashes into the ocean and everybody gets attacked by sharks.

"You don't have any experience with that, honey," my mother pointed out when I told her about it.

"Yeah, but I don't have experience with *anything*," I retorted. "It's not my fault I lead a boring life!"

"You could write about school," she suggested. "You're there five days a week."

I shook my head. "Too many characters. For every kid in the class, you've got parents, brothers and sisters, pet Chihuahuas, neighbors, maybe stepparents. Who wants to keep track of all those people?"

But even as I said it, an idea was taking shape in my head. What about *boarding* school? That would eliminate all the extra characters, because you *live* at the school! True, I'd never gone to boarding school, but I was sure I could fake it. I'd been to sleepaway camp— that counted as away from home. Put it together with school and you had *school away from home*!

The writing was just a blur. It unfolded almost like a movie in my head, and my job wasn't so much creating it as describing what I saw. It felt natural—like something I was always meant to do. At first, I worked on my project in class like everybody else. Pretty soon, though, that forty-five-minute period seemed like it was over before it had even started. The next logical step was to bring my notebook home and write at night.

I was having a great time, but it wasn't easy. It wasn't supposed to be. A lot of kids in my class joked that Mr. Hamilton came up with the novel idea because a track coach didn't want to have to think of a different writing assignment week after week. This was his way of saying, "Work on whatever you want for the rest of the year." Still, I think he knew what he was doing. The project forced us to follow our outlines until the story was finished. And most of us pushed on clear through to the end of the year in June.

The result was *This Can't Be Happening at Macdonald Hall!*— not just my novel for the assignment but my first novel, period. Mr. Hamilton gave me an A+ on it—although he also deducted one grade for messiness. So technically, I got a B+ on a book that's been around for more than forty years. (I was in middle school in the 1970s, long before you could write on a Chromebook or iPad. Penmanship—is that even a word anymore?—was something you got graded on.)

Sending my novel to a publisher wasn't a sudden flash of inspiration. The idea built slowly. It started when Mr. Hamilton offered to put a laminated version of my project in the school library. Even back then, teachers were compulsive laminators. That was an important message, though: *What you've written is good enough for people to read.*

Meanwhile, in room 124, the novels were all finished, and we were swapping projects and doing book reports on each other's work. Everyone who read mine said, "This is just like reading a real book from a bookstore."

Choosing a publisher was easy, mostly because I knew only one. I was the class monitor for Scholastic Book Clubs. That made me practically an employee, didn't it? Keeper of the bonus points—I had an *in*! Well, not really, but at least I had their address, which was printed on all the book order forms.

Then came the hard part—convincing my mother to type my novel out for me. Actually, she was really cool about it. But if she hadn't been, I might still be hunched over the manual typewriter, hunting and pecking. Remember—this was long before Word, before Google Docs, before spell-check, when every mistake meant blobbing Wite-Out clumsily onto the page. I probably would have given up and never become a writer.

A few words about the publishing business. Adults find it slow. For kids, it's glacier-speed. I stopped thinking about *This Can't Be Happening at Macdonald Hall!* a couple of weeks after I mailed it in. It took *four months* to hear back. And even then, the letter was so full of ". . . we might, possibly . . ." and ". . . if circumstances allow . . ." that I had trouble figuring out whether or not they even liked my novel.

My parents translated the adult into kid for me. It was a yes! I was going to be a published author! Looking back on it today, my life was quite literally changing before my eyes. The person I am now could never have existed if not for those few months of seventh grade. Those should be my greatest memories ever!

And how do I remember feeling about the incredible things that were happening to me? Lucky? Thrilled? Overwhelmed?

I was in *agony*.

I wrote the book in seventh grade, signed the contract in eighth, and by the time it came out, I had already started high school. Here I was, on top of the world, and all I ever did was *wait*. I waited for things that were taking *forever*. My impatience was like a monster that had swallowed me whole and was digesting me bit by bit. I couldn't even enjoy the success I'd had, because all I could think of was when, when, *when*?

If the waiting bugged me, revision was a double whammy. Not only did the whole editing process take centuries; it was also pure torture for me. I was an eighth grader when my first book went through revision, but I'm reasonably sure my editors thought I was a two-year-old in the middle of a hissy fit. I didn't just hate it—I was actually offended. Didn't these editors understand that every single word I chose was the best possible word in the English language to go in that particular spot?

It didn't help that *This Can't Be Happening at Macdonald Hall!* went through revision at the same time that all of Canada switched lock, stock, and barrel to the metric system. So while I wrestled with editors who were determined to undo my magnificent sentences, I also had to change miles to kilometers and Fahrenheit to Celsius. And even that was never as simple as it sounded. In one scene, I had a character inching his way across a windowsill. Can you *centimeter* your way across a windowsill? How weird would it sound when a sick kid took his temperature and moaned, "I'm burning up! I've got a fever of thirty-nine degrees!"

I was frustrated, aggravated, and stressed. In my mind, I was a kid who had written this amazing, flawless book (spoiler alert: it wasn't, but I didn't know that at the time). And along came this tag team of adults who were taking turns making it *less good* for no reason at all!

The irony is that I *love* working with editors today. Don't get me wrong—I still have hissy fits when editorial letters come in. Nobody wants to be told that what they've written isn't perfect. The message "Guess what? You thought you were done, but you've still got tons of work ahead of you!" isn't something anyone wants to hear. But over the years, I've submitted a lot of pretty mediocre first drafts that were bailed out by fantastic editors. Sometimes I don't even understand what my own story is about until I've fought with an editor over it. I'm totally serious—those arguments are an important part of making a novel as good as it can be. For the author, it's your first chance to see your story through somebody else's eyes. And the editor gets to hear what you were *trying* to do, even if you didn't totally succeed in the first draft.

If I had to give one piece of advice to my twelve-year-old self, it would be: "Chill out!" I was getting fan mail and doing TV interviews in ninth grade, but things like that only seemed to put me on edge. Getting my book published had landed me right smack-dab in the middle of the adult world, and I responded by turning myself into an overserious, overstressed adult. I was a funny guy. I wrote funny books. And I could be that person—for anybody but myself. Even now, more than forty years later, I still don't understand why I reacted that way.

Believe it or not, when I first found out that my seventh-grade project was going to be published, I wasn't that blown away. My friends all liked it. They were kids. It was a kids' book—what more could anybody want? It took decades in the book business for me to realize how fluky the whole thing had been. It was a miracle that anyone even read my manuscript. Scholastic's Canadian operation was a lot smaller in those days. *This Can't Be Happening at Macdonald Hall!* showed up in a pile of book orders. One of the warehouse guys noticed it and brought it—by *forklift*—to the offices where the editors worked. It would have been so easy for it to have ended up in a trash can somewhere. What were the odds that the first editor would even read a twelve-year-old's book? Or that he would love it and pass it on to his boss? Or she to hers?

At a reunion a few years back, an old acquaintance I hadn't seen since middle school noticed my name tag and exclaimed, "Gordon Korman—the last time I talked to you, you'd just signed a contract to publish a book for kids! What are you doing now, man?"

"Well," I replied, "last month I signed a contract to publish a book"—my face began to heat up as I realized how this must have sounded—"for kids."

It honestly seemed like I was caught in some paranormal time loop that had kept me stuck at a mental age of twelve!

Then I remembered an interview I'd seen with Mick Jagger, the lead singer of the iconic British rock band the Rolling Stones. It was the early sixties, right when the band was first formed, and a very young Mick proclaimed, "There's no way I'll still be singing 'Satisfaction' when I'm forty."

Mick's close to eighty today, a senior citizen, knighted by Queen Elizabeth. He's slowed down a bit, due to health issues. But guess what: the Rolling Stones still go on tour, and you can bet that they always play their most famous song, "(I Can't Get No) Satisfaction."

That makes me . . . almost . . . the Mick Jagger of kids' books! Not bad for a guy who started writing only because the track-and-field coach had to teach English.

I rolled my eyes along with everybody else that day in seventh grade when Mr. Hamilton first stepped into our English class. Little did I suspect *that* was the moment everything I was going to be suddenly became possible.

That's the thing about hope—sometimes it falls into place before you even know what it is you're hoping for.

GORDON KORMAN is a #1 *New York Times* bestselling author of books for kids and young adults, most recently *Operation Do-Over* and *Linked*. His writing career began at the age of twelve when a seventh-grade English assignment became his first novel. Now, four decades later, he is a full-time writer and speaker, with over thirty-five million copies of his books in print in dozens of languages. Each year he travels extensively, visiting schools and libraries, bringing his trademark humor and adventure styles to readers everywhere. This summer, Gordon will publish *The Fort*, his one hundredth book. A native of Ontario, Canada, he lives with his family in Long Island, New York.

I AM THE GREATEST

by James Bird

I met hope when I was three years old. It is one of my very first memories.
My mom and my brother, sister, and I were driving down the highway in Los Angeles late at night. We had just been evicted from our
apartment in Ventura and were heading to my uncle's apartment
in Watts to stay for a couple weeks until my mom could get a job
and save up enough money for us to get our own place. I was in the
back seat with my infant sister. My six-year-old brother was in the
front. It was around midnight. I should have been asleep but wasn't.
I was too confused. Hours earlier, I had seen a man in a uniform
yelling at my mom to grab what possessions we could carry and get
out of our home. And just like that, I didn't have a home anymore.
All my toys were on the sidewalk, in trash bags. What didn't fit
in our car was left near the curb. My mom was crying, and at the
time, I didn't know why. All I knew was that our car was making
funny noises and Mom kept begging it to get us where we needed
to go. Four more exits. Three more exits. Two more. And then it
happened.

Our car stopped. The radio turned off. The headlights went

black. We were stalled in the middle of the freeway at night. Our engine had had a heart attack. My sister was in a car seat, and I was strapped in beside her. We had just rounded a turn and weren't near any of the streetlights, so my mom knew the approaching cars would be blind to our location and would collide with us. At midnight, the only other vehicles on the road were huge semitrucks.

It took no time at all before a set of headlights lit up the wall behind us, quickly rounding the curve. The vehicle was coming fast. If it was in our lane, we were all about to be dead in seconds. My mom could have gotten out to save herself, but she knew there was no time to get all three of us out. Instead she turned around and said, "Hug me."

I reached out my arms to grab her. My brother hugged her side. She put one hand on my sister's tiny head, and she smiled. The headlights were so bright it felt like the sun was out. But then came a loud horn. Pressed and held down. My mom squeezed my arm and closed her eyes. I didn't close mine. I was still way too confused. I had no idea what was happening.

The next thing I remember was fireworks. And our car shook. It didn't explode and it wasn't crushed and launched into another lane. There was just a flurry of fireworks on one side of our car. My mom opened her eyes and mouth, but no words came out. But I did hear words. Words I didn't understand. Later in life, I'd realize these words were Spanish.

A white pickup truck pulled up beside us. Three men quickly jumped out. They checked on my mom and spoke to her. My mom was now smiling and crying again. These men must have been angels. Angels speak Spanish, and they drive trucks that have rakes and trash cans fastened to them.

These men risked their lives for us. They pushed as my mom steered our car to the shoulder of the freeway. My mom thanked them and kept crying, but they didn't have time to stay and talk. These angels must have had more stranded families to save. They called the police, hopped in their truck, and drove off.

My mom said that when she closed her eyes, moments before the semitruck turned the bend and, with no time to brake, pulled left as hard as it could to dodge our car, getting so close it scraped against the side and took out the driver's side mirror, she was hoping for so many things at once. Hoping the truck would miss us. Hoping we'd survive. Hoping if it did hit us, we'd all die quickly and not feel a thing. Hoping for a miracle. This was my introduction to hope. It was also the day I found out some cops are awful and will throw out everything you own onto the sidewalk, but some cops aren't. Some cops find families stranded on the side of the freeway and get you a hotel room for the night. My mom was too shaken up to tell this cop where we needed to go. He saw everything we owned was in our car. He put two and two together for the family of four and decided to help us.

The next morning, we walked alongside the LA River toward my uncle's apartment complex. And even at three years old, I knew that morning was special. It was the beginning of a new story. An unwritten one. Ours was supposed to end in a fiery crash of twisted metal. But we survived to see another chapter. My mom no longer had the eyes of an injured animal. She now had hopeful eyes. Like a mama bird that was ready to build another nest.

Our second shot at life wasn't any easier than the first. My mom was still raising three kids on her own. We were still poor. We bounced around from city to city, apartment to apartment, school to school, job to job, and there were two things that kept following us, no matter where we went. Hope and poverty.

We were always the poorest family around, even in places where everyone was poor. I knew this because kids my age always reminded me. You see, it's all about the shoes. Rich kids had shoes that said Nike, Adidas, or Reebok on them. Usually that meant they lived in a house and their parents had a car. Poor kids had shoes like Pro Wings or L.A. Gears. This meant they lived in an apartment. But my family didn't fall in either of these categories. We were often homeless. Even living in a car sometimes. And when we did get an apartment, we'd have to share it with a colony of cockroaches. This meant my shoes were hand-me-downs from my brother. They were often worn down and full of holes. I'd have silver duct tape wrapped around them to keep them intact. Those were my shoes. But here is where the hope comes in.

My mom turned being poor into an advantage for my brain. She saw how my brain worked unlike everyone's around me. She knew the way I learned was from stories, so she made up tales that made me forget about being poor. She told me that my shoes were more special than any pair of Nikes or Reeboks. Because on the silver duct tape, I could take a marker and invent my own shoes. A pair that no one else on Earth would have. Mine would be special. And it worked. I was proud of my shoes, even if they were falling apart. They were my Warriors, my Terminators, and since I was obsessed with reptiles as a kid, my shoes were often the only pair of "Alligators" in existence.

My mom used this tactic for many situations in my life. When other kids wore raincoats on rainy days, I'd have a black trash bag with a hole cut out to slip my head through. But those kids had to wear the same boring coat each rainy day. I didn't. I was special. I could throw mine out when I got to school, and when it was time to walk home, all I needed to do was visit the janitor's closet and get another raincoat. Mine were brand-new every day. And with duct tape, I was able to name my raincoats. Sure, all the other kids laughed and teased me about it, but deep down, I knew they were really jealous, like my mom told me they would be. Plus every time it rained and I was walking home, the city bus would stop and give me a free ride. I bet no other kids in their raincoats got free bus rides.

And no matter where we lived, my family was always the only Native American family around. This was a very important thing to know when I was younger because even when we had nothing—no home, no food, no car, and no money—my mom would whisper into my ear that everything and everywhere my eyes could see was mine. All these trees, hills, fields, houses, and buildings around us were technically ours. Everywhere my feet touched was my home. This made me feel rich. Even though I was getting older and realizing she was just saying these things to me to make me feel better. To give me hope. And so I'd pretend to believe her. I did it to make her feel better. To give her hope.

What is hope? Hope is like your shadow. When you find yourself in a dark place, you think it's gone. You think you're hopeless. Alone. But the moment you see some light, even if it's just a sliver, you realize hope is still there, right beside you, waiting for you to step forward so it can keep following you. Hope never leaves you. But sometimes hope doesn't look like hope at all. Sometimes it looks like victory, sometimes it looks like defeat. Here's a quick little story about how hope made me the person I am today.

One morning, when I was in seventh grade, I didn't want to go to school. I was crying and begging my mom to let me stay home. I hated school. I never wanted to go back. I told her that my brother was good at everything. He played sports and was always the best player. He got into fistfights and always won. He was even the best looking—all the girls would follow him around like he was a tall, handsome movie star. But me? I was the worst at everything. I sucked at sports. I was short. I got bad grades. I didn't win all my fights. There was something wrong with my brain, and everyone thought I was weird. Oh, and I had super-chubby cheeks. People my age were way smarter than me. I was always placed in the back of the class, even when I was in remedial classes. I guess you could say I was hopeless.

I wasn't good at anything. And I was sad all the time and spent hours alone in my room, listening to music, drawing, and writing "pooretry" (that's what I called poems about being poor). My mom saw I was down and figured out a way to "hope me up." This is what she did. She told me that she spoke to my Native American ancestors in a dream and that they told her they could prove to me that I was not only good at something, but I was the absolute best at something. Me? The best at something? No way.

This may have worked on me when I was much younger, but in seventh grade, I didn't buy it that her dreams channeled my Ojibwe-blood spirits and they told her this. (But also keep in mind that I was very sensitive, and to make my mom feel better, I decided to go along with it.)

"Prove it," I told her.

She said it would be a one-week battle, but at the end of the week, I would know what I was the very best at. This is how she proved it.

DAY ONE. MONDAY. My mom took me to a nearby park and

told all the kids that I was the fastest runner she'd ever seen and that I challenged them to race me. They took one look at me and agreed. *From here to the slides and back. Ready, set, go.* I ran as fast as I could. Faster than I would have ever thought possible. I imagined I was a cheetah . . . And guess what place I came in? Last. I said, "Let's go again." And we did. And again, I came in last. We continued this until they all agreed I was the slowest kid they'd ever seen, and they left the park. I told my mom that my ancestors were wrong. I lost every single race. But she reminded me it was going to take some time to reveal what I was the best at. It most certainly wasn't running.

DAY TWO. TUESDAY. My mom took me to the basketball courts after school. She told the other kids that I was the best basketball player she'd ever seen and could beat everyone one-on-one. They took one look at me and accepted the challenge. And just like the day before, every single kid there beat me. I challenged them all to a rematch, but they'd seen enough. I told my mom that all she was doing was proving I was the worst at everything, but she insisted that the week wasn't over. So, it wasn't running or basketball. But maybe tomorrow would reveal my strength?

DAY THREE. WEDNESDAY. At school, there was a spelling bee. My mom insisted that I enter it. She knew my brain was faulty when it came to words, math, and just about everything else school related. I couldn't even read a book because I would separate letters and vowels and make new words, so spelling for me was extra hard. But to make her feel better, I entered the spelling bee. Each student got their word. Some were right, some were wrong. And when it was my turn, they asked me to spell *satellite.*

My mom stood in the back of the class and gave me a thumbs-up.

I imagined a satellite up in space. But what I saw was a cowboy riding a giant flashlight.

I spelled it. *S-A-D-D-L-E L-I-G-H-T.* It made sense. The cowboy was riding the flashlight like a horse. Saddle light. I was sure I'd spelled it correctly and would move on to the next round, but they said I was wrong. I called them ridiculous and explained why I was right. They didn't know how to react to my logic, so they offered me another word. *Catastrophe.* I closed my eyes and imagined the word. I saw a cat. And the cat had a trophy in its hands. I smiled because like that cat, I was going to soon have a trophy. So, I spelled *C-A-T H-A-S T-R-O-P-H-Y.* Cat has trophy. And again, these bozos said I spelled it incorrectly. I argued again, but they ejected me from the spelling bee. Okay, so it wasn't running, basketball, or spelling. But only half of the week was through. I still had the second half to find out what I was the best at.

DAY FOUR. THURSDAY. My mom knew our neighborhood had a few kids I didn't get along with. They were the tough kids always getting in trouble with the cops. I was afraid of them because they were always fighting and breaking windows. She told me that this particular day of testing wasn't going to be easy, and it might even be a bit painful. But I never cared much about getting hurt—I was clumsy and had gotten myself injured all my life—so I told her to bring it on.

When the sun set and the night crept in, she took me down the hill and pointed to the kids smoking cigarettes and blasting music in their yard. I wasn't friends with any of them, but I knew who they were. Everyone knew. They jumped me and stole my skateboard the summer before. I told my mom I lost it, but she knew they had beaten me up because ever since then, I'd taken the long way home to avoid this area. I was particularly afraid of one of them: Chris Blake. He was the bully of the block. His street name was Casper. He was much taller than me and always walked around with no shirt on, because he had a six-pack. My mom approached them and said I wanted to challenge one of them to a fistfight, but the rules were that it had to be one-on-one. Winner kept my skateboard. My knees immediately began to shake. I was scared. I was hoping I'd be fighting the short, skinny kid. But just my luck, Casper was the one to accept.

My mom said I could quit at any time, even before the fight started, but I really disliked this guy and even though he was stronger, the thought of getting my skateboard back made me think a few bruises would be worth it. My brother beat me up a lot, so I wasn't too afraid of getting hit. I accepted the fight.

He was the first to throw a punch. And it hit me in the face, but I didn't register it. I was too busy telling myself to punch back. And I did. I hit him in the chin, and he stumbled and fell. He was stunned. Even I was stunned. He leaped up and tackled me, but my mom jumped in and broke up the fight before it went any further. I demanded a second round. I wanted to show this bully that I wasn't scared of my own neighborhood anymore. Chris refused to return my skateboard, since the fight was interrupted. But after that day, he never looked in my direction again.

I didn't win the fight. Nobody did. There's no way I could say I was the best. So, it was not running. Not basketball. Not spelling. And not fighting. I was sure my ancestors were wrong. And now I had a bruise under my eye.

DAY FIVE. FRIDAY. Like I said earlier, I had really chubby cheeks growing up. I hadn't hit my growth spurt yet, and everyone in school knew I was a bit off in the normal department, so having a girlfriend was pretty much an impossibility. But my mom said that in today's test I would ask out every girl I thought was pretty. That was a daunting task because I thought a lot of girls were pretty. But she convinced me that this test was given to me by the spirits of Ojibwe warriors and chiefs, who were the greatest human beings to ever live on Earth. So I agreed I'd try. If they are in my blood, that must mean I'm at least part great human being, right?

Well, this mission turned out to be much harder than fighting. I was terrified to talk to girls. But what's the worst that could happen—they'd say no? I'd been told no my entire life. So, during recess I walked up to Jackie, who was the prettiest girl in school, and asked her to be my girlfriend. She said no. I expected that. Her best friend Shelby was nearly just as pretty, so I asked if she'd like to be my girlfriend instead, but she also said no.

During lunch I asked out Dedra, Anna, and Alexis. They all said no. Anita was the only one to say maybe, but by the time school was over, she decided no. And I'll tell you what, the first few rejections hurt, but by the fifth, no, it didn't really feel like anything. It was basically on par with "Can I borrow a pencil? No? Okay." But asking a girl out wasn't as hard as I thought it would be. It was also obvious I wasn't the best. Not at running, basketball, spelling, fighting, or picking up girls. I went home and told my mom how they all said no, but she assured me not to worry. After all, there was still the weekend to figure out what I was the best at.

DAY SIX. SATURDAY. No school. My mom woke me up and handed me a box. It was full of useless items like picture frames, old toys, cassette tapes, used CDs, and magazines. She said that in today's test I'd go door-to-door in the neighborhood, trying to sell these items. How embarrassing (but that week had been very embarrassing already, so why stop now?). She told me that I should put in some of my toys as well. I refused, but she said not to worry because I didn't need to sell them, I just needed to bring them along. And since this disastrous test was almost over, I agreed.

I walked outside and began knocking on doors. Obviously, no one wanted the stuff, so I ended up selling them for nickels and dimes, even pennies. I guess my neighbors took pity on me and gave me whatever change was in their couches and pockets. By the time all the sellable items were gone, I saw the neighborhood kids playing handball in the alley. Our neighborhood was poor. It was called the Slater Slums. All that was left in the box were my toys that were not for sale. But I didn't need them anymore, and these kids didn't really have toys, so before I went home, I gave my toys to them, for free. I even gave all the change away to homeless people on the street.

When I returned, I had only an empty box to show my mom. I told her that I was the worst salesman alive. I actually lost money while trying to make money. She said that the test had shown that I'm not the fastest runner, I'm not the best basketball player, I'm not a champion speller, I'm not the best fighter, I'm not the world's greatest ladies' man, and I'm not the best salesman—but the next day would reveal what I am truly the very best at.

The rest of that day, I felt different than I'd ever felt. I realized some of those kids I ran with and played basketball against went to my school. And now I had a reason to talk to them instead of keeping my head down and eating lunch alone. Maybe I'd play basketball with them again. I also realized that I really liked words. Even though I spelled them wrong, they were fun little puzzles to put together. I looked up *satellite* and *catastrophe*. I even asked my mom for a dictionary. And told her if she didn't buy me one, I'd steal one to see if I was the world's greatest thief. So, that day she bought me my very first dictionary.

I realized I was no longer afraid to walk my own neighborhood. Chris Blake was basically afraid of me now. He knew I could take a punch and throw my own. I realized that that week I had talked to more girls than I ever had before. And maybe next week, I was going to ask a few more out. I also realized that giving my toys to those kids was far more fun than keeping them in my room, not being played with. Those toys were going to be loved, even though I couldn't sell a bottle of water to a man dying of thirst in a desert. I looked around my room and found more toys I could give away. I felt good . . . but I still had no idea what I was the best at. I guessed we'd find out the next day.

DAY SEVEN. SUNDAY. This time, I woke up my mom and asked her what my next test was. She said that she'd had another dream and one of the chief spirits was unable to watch my tests, so we had to do them all over again. I sighed and remembered everything I went through that week. All the losing. But to be honest, to find out what I was the best at, I'd happily do it all again. So, I looked my mom in the eyes and agreed.

That's when she said I passed the test. She said she knew what I was the best at. Seeing if I'd do it all over again was the final test. "Do you want to know what you are the best at?" she asked. "Yes," I said. And then she told me what it was. And the answer carried me through life and led me to where I am today.

And now I will tell you what I am the absolute best at. The truth is, I'll never be the fastest, the strongest, the smartest, or the most attractive guy. I'm an author, but I'm not the best author. I'm a director, but I'm not the best director. I'm a son, a father, and a husband, but I'll never be the best. But what I am the best at is this . . . Everyone gets knocked down. Everyone loses. Everyone. I don't care who you are or where you're from, rich or poor. In life, sooner or later, every single one of us will taste defeat. But I AM THE VERY BEST AT GETTING BACK UP. I lost every race and wanted more. I lost every game and wanted a rematch. I spelled the words wrong but wanted another word and made sure I got a dictionary for next time. I stood up to the bully. I was rejected by every girl, but the next week, I'd try again.

When it comes to getting knocked down and getting back up, I am the greatest. That is what my ancestor spirits told my mom. And they were right. So my challenge to whoever is reading this is to see if you are as good as I am at getting back up after being knocked down. Because if you never quit, you'll never fail. I've been knocked down a million times in life. But I've gotten back up a million times. I hope you never stay down. I hope you always get back on your feet and try again. And again. And again.

Here is what I've learned: Hope is a mother teaching her son a lesson that will shape him for the rest of his life. Hope is giving a toy to a kid who doesn't have any. Hope is giving change to someone who needs it. Hope is risking your life to help a family get safely off the freeway. Hope is standing up to the bully. Hope is picking up a kid dressed in black trash bags on a rainy day. Hope truly is everywhere if you look for it. Hope isn't something you do for yourself. It's what you do for others. To hope is to care. To care is to give. To give is to help. And to have hope for the future, we need to help one another right now. We are all in this together. *H-O-P-E*. I believe it stands for Helping. Other. People. Every day. Let's spread hope. Let's cover the entire planet in hope.

Speaking of hope, I hope that you read this and take me up on the challenge. Let's find out if you got what it takes. Your test begins now. And you should easily pass. I've already given you the answer. All you got to do is when you feel like giving up, don't. And when you get knocked down, get back up. And as often as you can, help someone. If you do these things, you will be well on your way to becoming the very *best*.

Love,
James Bird

JAMES BIRD is a Native American author of *The Brave* and *The Second Chance of Benjamin Waterfalls*. He's also an award-winning filmmaker, but his greatest creation is his son, Wolf.

BONES

by J.C. Cervantes

Mr. Hawkins drove a van with stickers all over it.
Mostly Grateful Dead.
He wore a scowl that made the deep lines of his tanned face look
like dried mud.

He was the school mystery.
No one knew anything about him.
Was he married? Did he have kids? Where did he grow up?
Why didn't he ever talk about himself?

He could hear the tiniest of whispers
across the classroom. He knew things,
things he shouldn't have.
Some kids thought Mr. H was an alien with eyes
in the back of his head.

He was different.
He did things no other teachers did.

He took the class on fossil excavations,
taught us about the building blocks
of the universe,
showed us what the inside of a frog looked like.

He had a thing for bones.
Even the kind you couldn't see,
like the bones of an idea.

Or the bones of a hope.
A dream.
Hopes and dreams have bones?

What did that mean?
I knew better than to ask. Mr. H would say,
What do you think it means?
Mr. H wanted you to figure things out on your own.

It was the library.

That's where I grew
the first bone.
In all those stories and spines.

The class went for an afternoon visit.
Mr. H planted himself in a corner chair, a level above
the rest of us
like a king or
a god.
He read a book with a black bird on the cover.

He never looked up. Not once.

He still busted
two kids who had been
messing around.

We all wanted to know
What did he say?
Are you in trouble?
They told us
He said something about opportunities.
Everyone cracked up.
        He said something about paying attention.
And not being able to hear

hopes and dreams.

That old man
is crazy.
Everyone laughed again. Even me, but deep down
I started to wonder if I
wasn't paying attention.

I went back to the library.
Again and again.

The librarian always let me
stay

for as long as I wanted
　　　　　hunting, absorbing, wondering.
Dreaming.

I checked the same books out
over and over and over.
Stories of magic.
Belonging.
And impossible odds.

Jenny, you have to give others a chance to read these.

But there was no one else in the library, and besides,
they weren't looking for the same
magic.

I read poetry,
mythology,
Shakespeare.
That was my secret.
My friends wouldn't understand.

I read
when no one was looking.
Once, I saw some of the same books tucked behind Mr. H's desk and
　　I wondered
if he kept them
a secret too.

I asked him about them.
He said something about doorways to new worlds.
He gave me books
to read.
After I returned them, he always asked,
How was the journey?

The words spoke to me,
the poetry *sang* to me.
I felt something
deep
deeper than bones.

Truth: I started
to write poems
to understand the world.

I once walked on clouds and breathed beneath the sea.
I knew how to fly until they told me what to be.

What to *be.*

So many voices telling telling telling.
The world doesn't work that way.
Don't waste your time.
That's a bad idea.
Girls don't do that.

It's *in the spines* I wanted to say.
In the bones.

Mr. H
he was different.
He said things like
Dream away.
You can be anything you want.
Just make the journey
worth it.

It was only
a small idea

Hidden there
in the pages of my journal
between the maybes and
what-ifs.

But whoever becomes somebody
when they live on a street that no one can pronounce?

I took the bus to the city library.
My friends liked to go for the deli across the street. Two-for-one
   BLTs
with extra bacon.

I looked up famous authors
studied their lives.

Did they know that they wanted
to *be* writers?
Artists?
Storytellers?

They lived in big cities.
They looked very serious.

They went to big schools.
Knew the right people.

Mostly men.
Sometimes women.

A bone.

But who says they want to be
a writer?
Too big. Too grand.

Too *Everything*.

I put Shakespeare away.
I tossed the myths
into boxes.
I did other things
to Belong.

Did you know
bones grow until you're twenty-five?
You can break them
and they heal.
Some say they grow back
stronger.

I've never broken a bone.
I saw it once.
Ugly, twisted—bloodied
flesh that screamed pain.

Before graduation
Mr. H told me to remember
the bones of
my hopes and dreams.
I promised.

But what if I wasn't born with the right bones, I wanted to say.

I got busy.
Sports, and beaches
and slumber parties.
I got busy
listening to music
I didn't like.
I tried on faces and voices and skin
that didn't fit.

I tried
to be like everyone else.

They seemed happy knowing
nothing about bones.

Why can't I be like them?

Every time I tried,
I broke another
bone.

Sometimes I would see
Mr. H's van in the old
school parking lot after hours and I'd pop in to say, *Hi.*
I worried
he'd ask if I had remembered
my promise.
If I had kept it, but
he never did.

He'd just show me
a new map or
book or fossil he'd collected.
It made me wonder,
When you were a kid, what did you want to be when you grew up?
He set the fossil aside.

Everything.

No one can
        be everything.

I can, he said.
Or at least
everything I wanted.

        How?

I'm a scientist,
an artist,
a mathematician, an engineer,
an archaeologist
all because I'm
a teacher.

        But
        what if it's too hard?
        What then?

He shrugged
pulled another book from his shelf.
Have you read this one?

A few years later,
Mr. H left that school.
I never saw him again.
I wished
everyone got a teacher as good as he was

at least once
in their life.

For years
I forgot him.
Left him on the grounds
of that school.

But in my mind,
he was always there,
in that classroom with his stacks of books,
his planet posters,
and piles of old maps. Looking at the world
through the eyes in the back of his head,
paying attention
to his dreams.

Here's the thing
about hopes and dreams—
they know how
to sleep.

> And they know when
> to wake up.

In college I wrote things.
Not stories.
Things about theories and arguments
and "great literature."
Things about dead authors: Dickens and Twain and Hemingway.

I read a line
by Maya Angelou:

There is no greater agony than bearing an untold story within you.

I wondered if the hard stuff,
the stuff we hide
is where our
true stories lie.

The stories we keep hidden
from the world,
because it's easier
to play small than
to dream big.

I wish
I still had the pencil
I used that day.
I didn't know those words would become
a book.

Hopes and dreams
they don't always come
fully formed.
Sometimes they arrive

in bits
and pieces,

like a puzzle you have to put together
over time.
Sometimes with the help
of many hands.
And sometimes

    it's too late
    to turn back.

Too late
because you've had a taste
of a new world
where you can be
    Everything.

The words came that day.
They poured out of me *every* day.

And the next day
    and the next
        and the next.

In those stories
I got to be
a witch,
and a baseball player,
a demon, and a god,
a broken-hearted teen,
and a hero.

I got to be
Everything.

When I began to teach English at the university,
I thought about Mr. H.
I knew he would like that I had figured it out
on my own.
The bones of my hopes and
dreams.

That I'd kept
my promise
after all.

That first day
I walked into the classroom
I began with these words,

We're going to start with the bones.

J.C. CERVANTES is a *New York Times* bestselling author of books for children and young adults. Her books have appeared on national lists, including the American Booksellers Association New Voices, Barnes and Noble's Best Young Reader Books, and Amazon's Best Books of the Month. She has earned multiple awards and recognitions, including the New Mexico Book Award and the Zia Book Award.

She currently resides in the Land of Enchantment with her family, three spoiled dogs, and a lifetime collection of books. But she keeps part of her heart in Southern California, where she was born and raised. When she isn't writing, she is haunting bookstores and searching for magic in all corners of the world.

THE DAY THE HOT DOG TRUCK CAME TO TOWN

by Max Brallier

For as long as I can remember, I wanted to be someone else.

Or, no, that's not quite right. It's more like—

For as long as I can remember, I wanted to be *someone* ~~else~~.

But not BE SOMEONE in that BIG way, like when some teacher says so-and-so is gonna grow up and really *"be someone!"*

I just wanted to be . . . some *one*.

One of a kind.

Although, hold on, pause—that's not exactly accurate, either. Because when a person is "one of a kind" it means that person is *wow*—a singularly unique and magnificent character. Like, "Remember Billy Mears? How he jumped the old ravine on that rusted Huffy, one training wheel still clinging to it, clanging away? Billy, man, Billy was *one of a kind.*"

No, I wanted to be one of a kind in the most literal way. In the way that there are *kinds* of things, I wanted to be a *kind* of person.

There are kinds of movies: comedy, action, horror. And kinds of candy: sweet, sour, chewy, hard.

And at some point during elementary school, I saw kids begin to fall into *kinds*: geeks, nerds, athletes, troublemakers, *cool* trouble-makers, took-it-too-far troublemakers.

In fourth grade, my kind was the *new kid kind*. I had moved to a new state, new city, and new school a few months into the school year. It was an awful *kind*.

Then it all got even worse. On that day in November when the hot dog truck came to town.

My dad wrote books. Not fiction, like I do now. He wrote books full of quotes, collections of trivia, compendiums of jokes. And when I was in fourth grade, he wrote *The Hot Dog Cookbook: The Wiener Work the World Awaited*. It was full of weird hot dog recipes: hot dog stew, hot dog birthday cake, hot dog lasagna, hot dog *everything*.

I was particularly aware of this book because it made our new house smell awful. See, my dad had to personally cook and eat every single weird hot dog concoction in the book.

"Why?" I asked.

"Lawyers," he answered.

My dad had to be sure none of his hot dog recipes would kill someone or make them barf or make their hair fall out. No author wants some ticked-off, barfy, prematurely balding customer racing back to the bookstore to return a cookbook.

The day the hot dog truck came to town, the final bell at school rang, like always. Kids were talking and joking and banging lockers and swinging backpacks. I was walking alone because that's what the *new kid kind* does.

As I shuffled toward the school's big swinging front doors, I became aware of hubbub. Action. Activity outside.

And then I heard my name. No one was talking to me—they were talking *about* me. First, a few kids saying, "Max." A few others whispering, "That new kid."

Then everyone was looking at me.

I didn't know why. I just knew it made me want to barf. Like I had just eaten hot dog gumbo (that's in *The Hot Dog Cookbook*, recipe 22, page 98).

I lowered my head, eyes on my sneakers, making my way through the front doors. A hill sloped down from the school. I looked. And at the bottom of the hill, parked directly in front of the school, was the Oscar Mayer Wienermobile. It was not big—it was HUGE. LONG AND SHINY, ORANGE AND YELLOW. A MASSIVE HOT DOG, so big it fully blocked out three houses across the street and, if I recall, partially blocked out the sun.

I *knew* before I actually knew. My name, my dad's stupid hot dog cookbook, and now a giant hot dog truck in front of the school. Couldn't be coincidence.

The big hot dog's door slid open like something on a flying saucer—and there was my dad. Waving. He couldn't have spotted me among the hundreds of other kids leaving the school—but in my memory, he does. He sees me and he's smiling so big and he's also sort of laughing because he knows how absurd and funny it is, and he knows he's surprised me good, and just thinking about it now, I feel that urge to barf starting to rush back again.

Someone said, "Hey, new kid—is that guy hanging out of the big hot dog your dad?"

"No."

"You sure? 'Cause the guy hanging out of the big hot dog is saying he's your dad."

I knew, then, what it must feel like to be a spy and have your cover blown.

"Nope," I said, and I spun around, saying something like, "I forgot my jacket," and I quick-walked through the school. A plan

57

formed, fast. The side hallway. At the end, a door. It led to the back parking lot. From there, I could sneak home. It was the long way home—but it was the only way home that would allow me to avoid that giant rolling hot dog monstrosity.

I made it to the back parking lot. Then to the street. Just two more blocks, then I could cut across the playground and slip into our backyard.

I didn't make it the two blocks. I didn't make it *two houses*.

The ground began to tremble. I can't promise it was exactly like this, it's too much like a scene from a bad musical—but in my head, I swear, it's *exactly* like this.

I looked back. The Oscar Mayer Wienermobile was rumbling up the street, coming toward me, massive, the vehicle's hot-dog-shaped front looking like the nose on a 747. Some dude barely old enough to have a driver's license behind the wheel, sporting a hot-dog-shaped hat.

And there was my dad, hanging out the side, waving, two hundred kids hurrying alongside.

All coming for me.

I was caught. If it were a bank heist, this was the moment when a dozen cop cars would pull up, sirens blaring, screeching to a stop from all angles. It's the moment when the thief-with-a-heart-of-gold has no place to run. It's all over. And the movie camera zooms in on his sad face.

I thought. *Okay, Max, you're caught. Only one option now: get in the hot dog truck, try to do it without barfing, demand the dude in the hot-dog-shaped hat drive away, fast. And after that, well, we'll have to move. Again. The whole family. Gotta blow town. New state, new city, new school. We'll need fake names. I'll need a new haircut. Possibly a fake mustache.*

I got in the motorized hot dog. All my classmates peered in. Kids poked the big wheels. They cheered, "Hot dog! Hot dog!" whenever its horn honked. It was the most exciting thing to happen in that town since Billy jumped the old ravine on that rusted Huffy, one training wheel still clinging to it, clanging away.

But the torment was not over!

We drove around town—for hours. The window was lowered, and I had to wave out it like I was the homecoming queen in a parade.

After that . . . still not over.

The Oscar Mayer Wienermobile parked in our driveway. *For two whole days.* And remember, we had *just* moved to this town. So, our neighbors thought it was our *actual car.*

"Hey, Betty, get a load of this," I imagined Mr. Saunders across the street saying, as he peered out his window. "The new neighbors . . . they got two cars. One's a baby-blue Chrysler. The other is A GIANT HOT DOG."

The next day at school, something was clear to me: in the end, there are really only *two kinds* of kids.

Kind #1: the kind that could revel in a thing like being picked up after school in a giant hot dog. The kind that could own it, laugh about it, tell the story again and again. The kind who's comfortable in his own skin. The cool kind.

And there was me, *Kind #2*, who hid in the bathroom stall and never wanted to talk about his weird dad or the weird hot dog vehicle ever again.

I so wanted to be *Kind #1*. Like the cool characters in the books and movies I constantly read and watched. And, man, I tried. For years. I was like Doctor Strange, wandering the globe in search for a cure for his mangled hands—willing to try *anything*.

Here, now, a brief and very incomplete list of ways I attempted to be *the cool kind*—

- Inform everyone at school that I was *very* afraid of snakes. Because Indiana Jones was afraid of snakes. And Indiana Jones was cool. Of course, the fear of snakes is not what makes Indiana Jones cool—it's the heroic action archaeology stuff.

- Proudly wear L.A. Lights, the original light-up sneakers. I convinced my parents to buy me a pair. I woke up early before school just to stare at them: shiny and fresh and clean. That first day wearing them to school, I must have gotten out of my seat about nineteen times to sharpen my pencil—any excuse to make those lights flash. Then, during lunch, I was informed by one of the actual cool kind kids that light-up sneakers were for fourth graders. And I was in fifth grade by that time. I missed it by one year.

- Act like an expert. I spent much of my seventh-grade field trip to Washington, DC, telling anyone who would listen that the Oakley sunglasses being sold on the corner were *not authentic* and they should *not* buy them. Because the kind of street-smart kid who knew the ins and outs of the world of knockoff Oakley sunglasses—that was a cool kind of kid.

- Rock the blackest of black jeans. For about nine months in 1995, black jeans were a big thing. A thing that a certain *kind* of kids—cool kids—wore. But the jeans couldn't *just* be black, they had to be really black, the blackest shade of black, like *black-hole* black. But my jeans were

only ever really black for, like, one day—and then my
mom would wash them and they'd turn a sort of chalky
gray. So, every night, I took a black Sharpie and applied
and reapplied Sharpie ink to every inch of my jeans. But,
during a particularly hot day in Ms. Switt's math class,
my sweaty butt stained the seat Sharpie black. I was
exposed! The blackness level of my jeans was phony—and
I was a phony, too.

None of it worked. I never succeeded.

After every failed day of being the *not-cool kind* at school, I went
home and sat in my tree house and read books in hope of forgetting
about my day's failures. And when the months got colder, I moved
inside, and I watched movies about heroes with buddies who had
great adventures and fought bad guys.

I'm now thirty-seven.

And you know what's the *most* embarrassing?

This little story-thing doesn't end with me accepting who I am.
It doesn't end with a big epiphany, me suddenly realizing, exclaim-
ing: "Being cool isn't what matters! What matters is being *you*! Being
true to yourself!"

Nope. I still *want* to be the cool kind. So bad. That *never* went
away.

I still have no idea what *kind* I am. I'm still not comfortable in
my own skin. I mean, I am who I am—that's the simple answer. But
I can't get my head around that.

But, and this is where I'm lucky: during all those years of trying
to be the cool kind, I never fully lost myself. The *Star Wars* nerd,
the comic book reader, the kid who hung out at the library after
school—I never destroyed that kid in my attempt to be the cool kind.

What I did learn, though, is that the *real me* exists and lives somewhere in between lots of kinds.

I'm not cool. And I never will be.

And I'm still the kind who'd be mortified to think that my dad might show up in front of the neighbors, trying to take me for a ride in a giant hot dog.

But now I'm also—a tiny bit, on a good day—the kind who'd be able to laugh about that.

MAX BRALLIER is a #1 *New York Times*, *USA Today*, and *Wall Street Journal* bestselling author. His books and series include The Last Kids on Earth, Eerie Elementary, Mister Shivers, Galactic Hot Dogs, and Can YOU Survive the Zombie Apocalypse? He is a writer and producer for Netflix's Emmy Award–winning adaptation of The Last Kids on Earth. Max lives in Los Angeles with his wife and daughter. Visit him at MaxBrallier.com.

SWEET SURPRISE

by Hena Khan

*The glass bowl was filled with milky pudding topped with crushed pista-*chios and fancy edible silver foil, and covered with a layer of plastic wrap. My mother and I carefully carried it into my second-grade classroom and presented it to Mrs. Powers, my gray-haired teacher. It was a special treat, my mother's savaiya, for an edible show-and-tell. The very best kind. I beamed while Mrs. Powers cooed her appreciation and took it to store in the staff lounge refrigerator to save for snack time later that afternoon.

The occasion was the Eid holiday. The day before, I had skipped school and visited the mosque for prayers dressed in my brand-new powder-blue and gold-embroidered gharara. There, I prayed with everyone, greeted friends and family, and collected a small wad of cash from adults. I spent the rest of the day feasting at the homes of friends on pudding like this, along with heaping plates of biryani, korma, and naan. Now I was going to share a delicious taste of the Muslim holiday, Pakistani style, with my lucky classmates.

I loved savaiya. It was cool and creamy. A thick, sweet pudding cooked with the thinnest vermicelli noodles. It's a tradition to wake up on Eid morning and have dessert for breakfast. And then again throughout the day. Different aunties put their own spin on the dish, but I preferred my mother's version. It was perfect.

It felt like eternity to wait until after lunch, and I was giddy with excitement when my class finally filed back into our room for snack time.

"Do you want to be a helper and serve everyone, dear?" Mrs. Powers asked me, handing me a stack of paper bowls. I nodded enthusiastically, excited for this moment. As I peeled back the plastic wrap, I smiled as a chorus of cheers erupted from the kids. But then, suddenly, the reactions abruptly changed.

"*Ewwww!*"

"*What is that?*"

"*Why does it smell like . . . perfume?*"

I caught a whiff of the pudding as I listened to them. It had apparently been scented with rose water. Unbeknownst to me, my mother had decided to add a surprise extra-special touch for this occasion.

One by one, the kids refused the bowls I tried to hand them. After the third or fourth attempt, Mrs. Powers gently stopped me from scooping out any more of the savaiya. It was clear nobody wanted to even taste the rose-scented dessert. Hot shame filled my face, and I blinked rapidly to stop tears as embarrassment gripped me. This was supposed to be a big moment, filled with pride, and it was totally ruined. Why in the world couldn't my mother have just made it the regular, un-special, unperfumed, and delicious way?

My mother was mortified when I angrily shared the story of

what happened later on at home. Despite my exasperated explanations, she simply couldn't understand why the kids didn't want the dessert. "But it's so tasty," she lamented, adding that she hoped the teachers ate it. As grumpy as I was about the entire situation, I didn't have the heart to tell her that the bulk of it probably ended up in the trash.

The moment passed, and I recovered from it, but from that day on, I never volunteered to share anything from my culture at school again. Over the years, I was quietly absent for Eid with no further explanation. I answered that my parents were from Pakistan when people asked me, "Where are you from?" but didn't choose to elaborate. And I gradually learned to separate my home life, my culture, and my religion from my school life. It just felt easier and safer that way. Besides, it never felt like anyone was really all that interested anyway.

Fast-forward to twenty-some years later. I was now the young mother of a three-year-old son of my own. One day, I got an unexpected call from my son's preschool teaching assistant, a sweet Pakistani lady named Mrs. Qadri.

"We are going to have a Ramadan party at school this Tuesday," she said over the phone. "Can you come?"

My initial reaction was glee. How different school life would be for my son compared to me! His own teacher was *hosting* a Ramadan party! It was inclusive and wonderful, and I was all for it.

"We can bring some treats for the kids," Mrs. Qadri continued. "Maybe some Pakistani sweet dish?"

"Um," I replied as my mind raced and I experienced a flashback to second grade and that day with the savaiya. I glanced at my son and decided he would not share the same fate as me.

"How about some Munchkins from Dunkin' Donuts?" I suggested, ignoring the disappointment in Mrs. Qadri's voice. The kids at Apple Montessori School would associate Ramadan with something safe and familiar. And my son would be proud of his holiday.

I arrived at the basement of the church where the preschool ran that afternoon, armed with two dozen doughnut holes in cardboard boxes. Before I even walked into the room, I was hit with another familiar scent from the motherland: not rose water this time, but the distinct spicy onion and masala blend of savory fritters called pakoras. Mrs. Qadri had her own ideas for the party, ideas that mirrored my mother's. I winced.

Don't get me wrong, pakoras are incredibly delicious. Put a big platter out in front of a crowd with a little chutney on the side, and they'll be devoured in minutes. But they are also irregularly shaped and have green bits of cilantro in them. To the uninitiated preschooler, they can be intimidating, like most new foods.

Mrs. Qadri didn't stop at pakoras, either. She'd also cut pieces of Pakistani sweets, colorful blocks of sweet cheese-like treats filled with nuts known as mithai, and arranged them on a silver tray. Those are a bit of an acquired taste for the non-desi palate. My heart broke for her as I predicted the reactions of the kids.

Sure enough, during snack time, the kids wrinkled up their noses and shook their heads as Mrs. Qadri walked around offering them the treats. I quickly followed behind her with the doughnuts— which were gobbled up—grateful I had them, even as the pinch of rejection of the traditional foods still hurt. I gorged on the pakoras myself and took some mithai to go so Mrs. Qadri would have to carry less of it home.

Mrs. Qadri, however, seemed unfazed. For story time, she

eagerly held up a few pages of paper she'd printed off the internet about Ramadan.

"Do you want to read this to the kids?" she offered. I hesitated, unaccustomed at that time to reading or presenting to a group of kids.

"Why don't you go ahead?" I said.

Mrs. Qadri went on to read from her pages about the meaning of Ramadan. In a group of fifteen preschoolers sitting crisscross applesauce on the carpet, I winced again as she recited, "Ramadan is a holy month in Islam, a commemoration of the Prophet Muhammad's first revelation, and its observance every year is regarded as one of the five pillars of the religion."

It was an accurate description but also painfully boring and confusing for her young audience. She was barely past the opening paragraph when their eyes glazed over. They lost interest and started to roll around on the carpet, poke each other, or wander away.

In that moment, the idea for my first picture book, *Night of the Moon*, popped into my head. I decided that I would write a story that would showcase the joys of Ramadan and Eid from the perspective of a child. I'd make sure that it was vibrantly illustrated and appealing to kids. And I would leave out mentions of revelations and pillars and instead talk about delicious foods, parties, new clothes, and presents—things everyone could relate to and understand.

In that first book, I mentioned the practice of fasting, the importance of gratitude, the role of charity, and more. But along with things like kabobs and milky pudding, I included chocolate fudge cake. And along with henna tattoos, I wrote about trampolines. Because here in America, kids like mine experience all of these things in our celebrations, which have evolved into a beautiful blending of cultures.

It was amazing to see my first book be published and make its way into libraries and schools. A bunch of Ramadan books followed in its path, including another I wrote called *It's Ramadan, Curious George*. I grew emotional while imagining Curious George celebrating Ramadan with his Muslim friends. And I figured something like that could seriously get kids of all backgrounds hyped, or at least hold their attention long enough to sit through the whole story. Ultimately, it got an even bigger reaction than I expected from people of all ages who had hungered to be seen and included by a major brand. It meant more to my community of American Muslims than I had realized.

When I look back on the past, I now fully appreciate the efforts of people like my mother and Mrs. Qadri. They're so sincere in their desire to share, and so close to the experiences they are sharing, that they can't fathom why others don't always appreciate their efforts. As a self-conscious kid straddling two cultures, though, I could see both sides. I understood why children might dismiss something new as weird or gross. It didn't sting any less in the moment, but it made sense to me.

I'm grateful for those experiences now, because they taught me empathy, sensitivity to what it feels like to be on the outside, and more. And the funny thing is that now I'm the total opposite of who I was as a kid. Fast-forward a few more years to today, and I absolutely love sharing about my culture, religion, and traditions. Apart from my picture books, I also write novels about kids like me and mine. In them I weave Pakistani foods, clothing, games, and traditions throughout the stories. I blend in Muslim holidays and scenes that include the call to prayer and the mosque. And I honestly can't imagine *not* including these things.

At the same time, I still wish that I'd had those types of books for myself when I was growing up. I can only guess how much more confident I might have been if I had walked into my library or classroom and seen them sitting on the shelf. They would have told me: "You belong," and "Your life matters." Maybe I would have better understood that even though some of us have different languages, customs, traditions, religions, and families, there's so much more that we have in common with one another. Some of us might enjoy rose-scented pudding, while others prefer doughnuts. But we all love sweet treats, celebrations, and presents.

I'm always amazed and happy to meet kids who are so far ahead of where I was at their age. So many are proud of their heritage and don't seem to get embarrassed in the same way I did when I was younger. Many have learned the meanings of terms like *culture*, *ethnicity*, *race*, and *identity* and understand how they apply to their lives. Most are genuinely curious and respectful toward those who are different from them.

But every now and then I meet someone who reminds me of younger me, kids who still seem a little uncomfortable in their own skin. Maybe they've had moments that have been awkward or uneasy, and they've left a scar. If that's you, I promise that one day others will appreciate the unique things about you that make you who you are. And eventually, you will, too.

In the meantime, I hope everyone reading this will try a pakora or some savaiya, or something else new you've never tasted. I hope you'll pick up a book about a person from a background that is unlike your own. It might feel strange at first, but I think you'll be surprised by how delicious and familiar you find it in the end.

HENA KHAN is the award-winning author of the middle grade novels *Amina's Voice*, *Amina's Song*, and *More to the Story*, and the Zayd Saleem, Chasing the Dream and Zara's Rules series. She wrote several pick-your-path books, including the Super You! series, and a bunch of picture books like *Golden Domes and Silver Lanterns* and *Under My Hijab*. Hena lives in Maryland with her family but is grateful to be able to travel a lot. Her favorite things are reading in bed, perfect cappuccinos, and getting letters from kids.

LETTER TO MY DAUGHTER ON HER EIGHTH-GRADE GRADUATION

by Pablo Cartaya

Hey!

Before you dive in, I wanted to touch base and explain why I chose to write a letter to my daughter for this anthology on hope. If you're reading this, you probably know about the global pandemic that uprooted much of the world. You, or someone you know, was probably affected in some impactful way. It was a tough time. The world seemed to be caving in on itself. It was *rough*. To be honest, I don't know how much better things are right now. Maybe better. Maybe good. Maybe not.

In March 2020, my daughter Penelope went from going to school to complete virtual learning literally overnight, and her school stayed virtual through June 2021. She didn't have an eighth-grade graduation ceremony, nor a dance, nor even a place to hang out safely with her friends. She lost three grandparents that year. Her mother got sick. Her baby sister got sick. She saw her little brother celebrate his birthday via Zoom.

The anxiety, loneliness, and fear she felt was something I'll never forget. But as I watched her through that difficult year, she taught me something amazing. It's a lesson I will never forget. This letter is my reflection on that lesson. Writing does that. It allows us to put words together to form a thought that can later become a story—or in this case, a letter . . .

· · ·

My dearest Penelope,

You've been through so much these last three years. Some of middle school was pretty great. Some of it was just *blah*. Some of it, I know, sucked. But in the end, you closed your laptop on your last online class and smiled (braces off) while you told me, "I'm ready for high school, Papa."

Yes, you most definitely are. But first, please allow me to reflect on these last three years . . .

I remember when you walked into your sixth-grade class. You were shorter than most of the other kids. There was a wide-eyed curiosity about everything that lay ahead. You were nervous, excited, hopeful. You had pigtail braids. You hadn't yet gotten your braces— that would happen a few months later. I remember sitting in the orientation of your theater class and watching as you looked around trying to figure out who was going to be your friend.

You made a few friends in sixth and then some new ones in seventh and then some new ones in eighth. They were all different, and it showed me how you're capable of having many different kinds of people in your life. You don't follow a particular group; you just follow your heart and who makes you happy.

You've taken every challenge and processed it and broken it down and then gone for it. No matter the circumstances. And we can safely say there were some circumstances!

I mean, right when you were about to finish seventh grade, the whole world shut down. Suddenly, all these online classes popped up, and nobody had any idea how to navigate them. Not students. Not teachers. Not parents. Not even our government!

The way you adapted to online learning and how, in spite of not being given the accommodations you needed, you still managed to pull through and thrive in an environment nobody was prepared for—not even your parents.

Like math.

The way you patiently waited while I tried to explain geometry only to find out I was logged in to the wrong math class the entire time. The way you couldn't get a decent math teacher to ever understand that math is *difficult* for you and it's not that you're being lazy! I get it. I wasn't exactly in love with math at your age, either.

You took it all in stride. You continued to work hard and try to understand. You got frustrated when you saw me get frustrated, and then you softened up when you saw how stressful everything had become.

Our little house was suddenly flush with Momma at home, and your brother, and your baby sister, and your dad trying to navigate deadlines and math that he hadn't done in over twenty years—and even when he did study it, he still wasn't very good at it.

You understood that your frustration was not singular—that many people were struggling like you were. That the world was suffering.

The world had changed overnight, and you stood up and demanded something must be done. You grew into your social activism and were unafraid to show who you were and how the world needed a reckoning, and that you were there for the fight. I saw how you began to see the world through the eyes of others. Through the eyes of injustice and your increasing rage at intolerance.

I saw how in quarantine your little brother was crying in his room because not even Abuela could see him on his birthday, and you invited him for a "sleepover" and let him watch whatever movie he wanted.

I saw how you began to ask us questions about the world. Asking for answers and measuring our responses—almost like testing us to make sure we understood the position you took—on everything from social justice to human dignity to why we needed to watch *My Hero Academia*.

I saw how you rolled your eyes when we went hiking in the mountains to escape the brutal Miami summer (I have videos of that face). You standing on the ledge overlooking the beautiful landscape with a look that said—*Why the heck did you make me go on this two-mile hike in the middle of these woods?*

I also saw the face you gave when we reached our destination, and the humid air gave way to the cold as the mountain left remnants of winter at its base. Enough for a teenager to abate her frustrations and marvel at the beauty of nature.

You've never been afraid to apologize. That's a gift. Believe me.

You're a lightning bolt inside a peony. Everything about you is beautiful, powerful, electric. Your strength, your tenacity, your spirit always amaze me. The way you take care of your siblings and also demand respect from them, and from everyone who comes into your orbit. From the second you came into this world, you've proved time and time again that you are a force to be reckoned with.

I'll never forget the moment you came into this world.

The emergency C-section. Watching Momma shaking on the cold hospital table. Wondering what was wrong. Then the doctor took you out—"right on time," she said—and I nearly lost myself.

I looked on, a combination of fear and hope as they pulled your tiny purple body out. You dangled there for a moment. The doctor tapped you twice on the chest and after less than a second, you sprang to life and let out a cry that filled the cold room and warmed my worried heart. From that moment on, you would constantly prove to everyone that you are someone who not only survives under great pressure—you thrive.

You learned to love stories. Using your audiobook device and flipping the pages of the physical book at such a rate, I found it difficult to keep up with what book you were reading and when. The loud crying from your room when a favorite character died, or the sheer joy when two characters you totally "shipped" at the beginning of the novel miraculously got together in the end.

You spent the last three years in middle school figuring yourself out, and I want you to know how proud I am of everything you've had to overcome to get yourself into high school and ready for the next journey of your epic adventure.

Watching you go through the many ups and downs of a really tough time in your life and managing to get through with such triumph is inspiring. *You* are an inspiration. *You*. Give me my greatest hope.

I want you to know . . .

. . . sometimes we fall. Sometimes we feel like the world is caving in on us. Like it's hard to breathe and there's no place to get air into our lungs.

I want you to know . . .

. . . I've also felt like that before. I've also known what it's like to finally catch that breath. To feel my lungs fill with oxygen.

I want you to know . . .

. . . sometimes all we need to do is breathe and recognize the air was there all along.

I want you to know . . .

. . . I worry about you. I was scared when they called your mom and me from the school to say you needed to go to the hospital. It scared us, but I'm grateful you were okay.

I want you to know . . .

. . . I was not mad. Neither was Momma. We were just scared. Middle school sucks sometimes. I already told you this, but it bears repeating.

I want you to know . . .

. . . your resilience is what inspires me to be the best at my job and to be there when you need me. To be a champion of you and everything you do.

I know you've been bullied because you're different.

Looked down on because you are trying to be you.

But I also know you erased those negative influences from your sphere and commanded they would never, ever have dominion over you again.

You are brave beyond measure.

You are caring and compassionate.

And I see in you everything I wish for this world.

I still have the poem you wrote just before you entered fifth grade. With your permission I'm going to repeat it here:

I see a smile in the sun
Sometimes the sun is talking to me
And it says. You're a happy girl.
The sun makes me Love ideas.

Ideas like how to be kind.
When it rains.
Clouds cry.
So the Sun.
Tries to brighten them up.
With happiness!
Sometimes the sun's talking to me.
And it says you're a happy girl.

And do you remember this other poem? The one you wrote about your friend who was having a tough time in school.

Abby
I think clouds are shy
Why do I?
Well because
Sometimes I see clouds get pink
And I think.
Whenever you look at them.
They blush.

And so here I am, writing this on your last day of eighth grade, and all I can think is how lucky I am to be your dad. I want to tell you that you are, and have always given me, so much hope for the world. So much promise. My greatest joy is that I've gotten to witness the world next to your eyes, your voice, and through your stories.

As you head off into summer and prepare for high school, I want you to know how much hope I have for everything you are and will be.

I want you to know

I love you.

And I want to thank you for sharing the gift that is you.

Te quiero con todo mi corazón,
Papa

PABLO CARTAYA is an award-winning author, screenwriter, speaker, and occasional actor. He is the author of *The Epic Fail of Arturo Zamora, Marcus Vega Doesn't Speak Spanish,* and *Each Tiny Spark.* His forthcoming titles include *The Last Beekeeper,* a middle grade novel that contemplates a future where bees are central to rebuilding the world, and *¡Leo! El Magnífico,* an Apple+ Ghost Writer Series novel. His novels primarily focus on the themes of family, community, and culture. He lives in the hyphens between his Cuban and American identities and with his familia in Miami. Visit him at PabloCartaya.com.

HOPE IN THE HALLS OF CATHOLIC SCHOOL

by Karina Yan Glaser

Hope wasn't something I spent a lot of time thinking about when I was growing up. If I had a word to describe childhood, it would be *survival.* I know a lot of people can relate to that. Growing up, I changed schools almost every year. Already a shy kid, I found changing schools every year to be pure torture. However, all that change taught me a very useful trick: invisibility. I spent a lot of time in school libraries, hidden in the stacks, content to spend recesses and lunchtimes with familiar books.

The year I entered sixth grade, I (surprise, surprise) entered a new school. It was a Catholic school, and I didn't even know my mom had put in an application for me to attend until a couple of weeks before school started. I had taken a test to get into this school, but I remember thinking it was a test to get into our public school's gifted program. My teachers tested me for gifted programs every year since I was a good student, but I never scored high enough to get in. I was not very good at standardized tests. All I can recall is one day in late August before sixth grade, my mom brought me to a building that had a gigantic cross in front of it. Our family wasn't religious, so that was a surprise.

"We are buying uniforms," Mom informed me. "This new school makes you wear uniforms."

"A uniform?" I gaped.

I had gone only to public schools in the past, and at all of those schools I could wear whatever I wanted. Or, I wore whatever my mom made me wear. I distinctly remembered going to school in terry-cloth shorts when I was in first grade. When I entered the schoolyard where we gathered in class lines before school began, everyone pointed at me and yelled, "Short shorts! Short shorts!" When I came home and told my mom about it, she shrugged.

"Those are the style shorts I wore for school in Hong Kong," Mom said.

I refused to wear those shorts again, even though they *were* comfortable. Instead, I wore jeans like everyone else and suffered through the California heat.

At least now, with the uniform, I wouldn't have to worry about wearing the wrong thing to this new Catholic school. Mom led me past the cross and into the building. We entered an auditorium that was filled with tables. On top of the tables were rows of folded-up clothes. A woman whose blow-dried hair easily gave her an extra three inches of height welcomed us.

My mom pointed to me and said, "She is a new student here."

The woman smiled, asked me what grade I was going into, and led me to one of the tables.

"There are three different color pinafores," the woman explained, pointing to the light yellow, light blue, and light pink jumpers. "Underneath you have to wear a blouse." She pointed to a blouse with an elaborate collar, what I imagined someone would wear in Victorian England. One side of the collar was embroidered with swirly script. The woman explained that the monogram was of the school's initials.

My mom bought me one pinafore in each color and a few blouses. The woman with the hair led us to another table with navy-blue shorts and white shirts. These were the PE uniforms, and the shorts were very much like those unfortunate shorts that made everyone laugh at me back in first grade! Life had truly come around full circle.

Armed with cotton-candy-colored pinafores, Victorian blouses, and PE shorts like those my mom wore when she was a child, we headed home. Two weeks later, school began. I returned to the building with the huge cross, only this time I was wearing a yellow pinafore that went well past my knees. Since I was new, someone from the front office showed me where to wait. She led me to a group of girls who were also in sixth grade. And . . . none of them were wearing yellow pinafores. Some kids were wearing the pink ones, but most of them were wearing blue! I slowly turned around, taking a closer look at the rest of the school, where hundreds of kids were milling around the courtyard waiting for the school bell to ring.

Not one person was wearing a yellow pinafore.

"You must be new," a girl with a white bow in her blond hair said to me.

I nodded, noticing that she was staring at my pinafore with sympathy. I looked back at her and noticed that her hemline was much, much shorter than mine. It was at least three inches above her knee! And her blouse didn't have an elaborate collar. Hers was a crisp, white blouse with no school monogram.

I felt betrayed by the uniform lady, who had led me astray in every way. It was as if I was back in first grade, when everyone was pointing at my short shorts and laughing.

My transition to sixth grade was definitely the most difficult out of all my school transitions, and not just because of the uniform. Most of the students had been at the school since preschool, so there were friend dynamics that I didn't understand and coursework I had never learned. I got a D- on my first science test because the majority of the questions were review from the previous year. On the first non-uniform day of the school year, everyone in my class wore a special brand of T-shirt that turned colors in the sun. I had never seen shirts like this before. There was obviously an unspoken code about clothes that I knew nothing about.

Furthermore, the class I entered was very heavily skewed toward boys. Two-thirds of the grade were boys. Maybe I, a non-Catholic, was accepted into the school in the first place only because they needed more girls! There were sixteen girls total, and they were split into two main cliques. One group liked sports and school, and the other group liked makeup and boys. I was in a third group, all by myself. I was the one who went to the library and read during recess and lunch.

One of the biggest changes was being at a Catholic school. I had never been exposed to religion, so seeing crosses and artwork of Jesus and Mary at every turn was a real eye-opener. There was mass every Friday, and everyone took communion. I had no idea what communion was, and when I asked the teacher, she said it was the body and blood of Christ. That made me incredibly uncomfortable. Thankfully, I wasn't allowed to take communion, because to do that you had to have been baptized in second grade. Instead, I was told to cross my hands over my chest, and when I got to the priest, he thumbprinted a cross on my forehead. The only other kids in the school who had to cross their hands over their chest were the kids younger than second grade.

But hope comes in small and unexpected ways. A month after school began, a girl in the sports-and-school girl clique asked if I wanted to walk to class with her. The next thing I knew, I started hanging out with that group at lunch instead of hiding in the library. When they found out I was a gymnast, they begged me to show them what I could do during recess.

"But I'm wearing a dress," I said, gesturing at my blue pinafore. (I never again wore the yellow one after the first day of school.)

"Don't you wear shorts underneath?" one of the girls asked. She flipped up her skirt to reveal plaid boxer shorts, the kind that boys wear as underwear!

"I'll wear something tomorrow," I promised her.

When my mom picked me up later that day, I told her I needed boxer shorts.

"Why?" she said, horrified.

"Mo-om, please!" I begged. "I have to wear something under my dress so I can do sports with the other kids during recess."

"Wear your PE shorts," Mom told me, as she drove us home. She did not stop at the store to buy boxer shorts.

It turned out that no one cared that I wore PE shorts under my pinafore. What they did care about was the way I could flip and tumble on the grass. And slowly, I began to fit in more. I was invited to birthday sleepovers and introduced to rollerblading (I was terrible at it) and TP'ing the houses of boys in our class late at night (I never understood the point of that) and shaving my legs (my mom was not very happy to see all the cuts I came home with). For my birthday, even though I didn't have a party or a sleepover, a few of my friends came to school with gifts. Inside one of the wrapped packages was that elusive T-shirt that changed colors in the sun.

I was shocked when I didn't have to switch schools for seventh grade and even more shocked that I stayed at the same school in eighth grade. I had never stayed in the same school that long before. By then, I had gotten used to Catholic school and no longer shuddered at the images of Jesus nailed to the cross hanging in every hallway. I had joined the school sports teams and learned how to play volleyball, a sport I had never heard of before.

Eighth grade was the final year at that school; we would all be moving on to different high schools after graduation. One of the big events of the last year was the eighth-grade musical. It was a Big Deal, which I knew from watching the eighth graders perform it when I was in sixth and seventh grades.

There was a buzz in the air the day the music teacher was going to tell us which musical we would be doing. We held our breath as we waited to find out the selection. Finally, it was announced.

We were doing *The Adventures of Tom Sawyer*.

Tom Sawyer! All the girls looked at each other and sighed. We knew they had selected a musical that had a lot of boy leads because there were so many boys in our grade, but it was still a disappointment. There was only one lead girl part in the whole musical: Becky Thatcher. And nearly every girl in the grade was going to audition for the part, including me.

Even though I had learned a lot about the school culture in the past couple of years, I underestimated the ruthlessness around the eighth-grade musical. Getting a good part was a badge of glory, it seemed. On the day of auditions, while all the other girls auditioning for Becky paced around the classroom mumbling lines to themselves, I sat with the script on my lap and took deep breaths. To me, singing a song and saying some lines was a lot less stressful than doing flips on a balance beam that was only four inches wide. We were all auditioning at the same time, just standing up when our name was called and singing the one song Becky had a solo in. When my turn came and the pianist started up the jaunty tune, I took a deep breath and belted out, *"Ain't nothin'! 'Cause I'd druther go a-fishin' with you!"*

Honestly, I was surprised that I could sound so loud and in tune. Our music teacher looked surprised, too, as did the other kids in my grade. I was known for being pretty quiet, my teachers often asking me to speak up in class. I guess all that singing practice in the shower was useful for something.

In the end, I got the Becky Thatcher part. The other girls in the class were resentful at first, but then we discovered that Becky had to kiss Tom in the musical, onstage, in front of everyone! The guy chosen to play Tom was not particularly well liked, so I think the other girls felt as if they had dodged a bullet.

The first time we practiced the kiss was in front of the whole eighth grade, who, in the fashion of thirteen- and fourteen-year-olds, were completely immature about it. There was much laughing and hooting and teasing. I fled the stage afterward in embarrassment. But, besides the kissing scene, being in the play was a lot of fun. I loved the feeling of being backstage, waiting in the wings for a scene to begin, stage lights illuminating the set and a quiet expectation filling the auditorium.

It is not lost on me that the first glimpse of hope I felt at the new school was an invitation from someone to join them. It's funny how one invitation can change so much, but it did. I still remember it now, decades later, when I see someone enter an unfamiliar place for the first time. I know what it's like to be new and invisible and uncertain, and I know how much it means to have someone reach out.

So now, when I have an opportunity to welcome someone into a new situation, I walk over, just like my friend did so many years ago, and I extend a hand. I extend hope.

KARINA VAN GLASER is the *New York Times* bestselling author of the Vanderbeekers series. She is a contributing editor for Book Riot and lives in Harlem with her husband, two daughters, and an assortment of rescue animals. One of her proudest achievements is raising two kids who can't go anywhere without a book. Find her online at KarinaGlaser.com.

HELPFUL TIPS FOR
THE WORST WEEK OF YOUR LIFE

by Stuart Gibbs

This is a sad story, but it has a happy ending.

On the first day of March in 2018, I went to an event to celebrate the release of *Hope Nation,* the book that preceded this one. I had been friends with the editor, Rose Brock, for years and wanted to support her amazing project. I listened to the writers Atia Abawi, Nicola Yoon, and Marie Lu each speak about adversity they had overcome. I met the wonderful writer Julie Buxbaum, who subsequently became a close friend. Afterward, Rose and I went out for Mexican food. It was a lovely evening.

That night, Rose told me about the book that you are holding in your hands right now. She asked me if I would write an essay. My immediate response was to tell Rose that I had nothing to write about. It's not as though my life has been completely free from adversity. And yet, I am a white man in a culture that gives white men advantages most other people don't have. My parents have always been loving, caring, and supportive. I have a wonderful relationship with my sister. I have managed to get a career doing something that

I love. I have a large group of friends. I have been able to travel all over the world and have amazing experiences. I have never had to fight in a war or live under an oppressive government. I haven't battled cancer or ALS or addiction.

So I told Rose that I should probably pass on writing a piece. "I've never had to overcome anything," I told her.

Less than a month later, my wife died.

It shouldn't have happened. She'd had a routine surgery, and things went wrong afterward.

It was devastating.

But I think it was probably even worse for my children.

My son was only twelve at the time, and my daughter was just about to turn ten. There is certainly no good time to lose a parent, but I think those ages are particularly fraught. Younger kids might not have grasped the enormity of what had happened. And of course, as you get older, the death of a parent is part of the natural course of life.

But losing a parent when you are a tween is just awful.

It was a terrible, horrible twist of fate, and my kids knew it. They knew they had suddenly been dealt a terrible hand. They knew it was unfair. They knew it was cruel.

And they couldn't do anything to change it.

To be honest, I can't tell you exactly what my children went through. Every single person experiences grief differently.

Although I can tell you a few things that helped.

The way I figured out how to get through my grief was to try to figure out how to help my children get through *their* grief. But a lot of the time, the tools that worked for them worked for me, too.

I really, really hope you don't ever have to go through something tragic in your life. Obviously, at some point, you are going to lose a loved one, but I hope that it happens in the natural course of events, and that the death isn't sudden and devastating. But if that happens, maybe what I'm about to say here will help you, too.

1. DON'T GO THROUGH IT ALONE.

Talk to people. Hopefully, you have family and friends you can confide in. (Although, I realize, it's possible that you might have just lost your closest confidant.) Let them into your life. Let them help you. Don't be afraid to tell them what you need, whether it's a game of catch or a sandwich from your favorite deli or just a hug. (Hugs when you are grieving are really important.)

Fun fact: several of the other writers of essays in this book were among the many people who helped me. They were there to talk on the phone, offer advice, and offer those hugs I mentioned. At the time of my wife's death, I was only just getting to know some of them, but they would become very close friends over the ensuing years.

And while I'm on the subject of talking to people . . .

2. THERAPY IS NOTHING TO BE ASHAMED OF.

I know that in many places, there is a stigma about therapy. Where I grew up, telling people you went to therapy was like saying that you believed in unicorns. Which is a shame, because therapy is incredibly helpful. Therapists can help you handle the loss of a loved one, help you deal with your parents' divorce, or possibly even convince you that there are no such things as unicorns. My children and I have all seen therapists individually—although some people prefer group therapy. There are even summer camps for kids going through grief. And if you fear that a therapist will cost too much money, you should know that in most cities, there are options for therapy that are free, supported by generous donors.

3. DON'T BE AFRAID TO TALK ABOUT THE PERSON WHO DIED.

This might seem odd to say, but a lot of people don't do this. Perhaps they find it awkward to talk about someone who just died. Or maybe they think it's wrong to do so. I have heard many stories of families in grief who never even spoke about the deceased family member, almost as if they had never existed. This would not be a positive behavior . . . And yet, I can see why some people might do it.

Right after my wife died, I found myself unsure whether or not I should share stories about her with my kids—because I feared those stories would upset them. But you know what? They never did. My kids always appreciated the stories. I even asked my therapist if this was the right thing to do. She told me, "You never want to pretend that the person who died never existed." So if you're grieving—or helping a friend through grief—it's nice to share stories about the person who died.

4. BE PREPARED. PEOPLE ARE GOING TO SAY THE WRONG THINGS TO YOU.

Frankly, no one knows the exact right thing to say to someone who is grieving. Because everyone is different. What is right for you might not be right for someone else. And so, there are going to be things that people say to you that, no matter how well meaning, still set your teeth on edge.

I'll tell you mine. I *hated* when people told me, "I'm sure your wife is up in Heaven, looking down on you." And here's why: It seemed to me that, if my wife was in Heaven, the *last* thing she'd want to be doing would be looking down on us. Because all it would do was remind her that we were going on with our lives without her, which would certainly be upsetting to her. If anything, my wife would have been much happier going to a spa all day. But no one ever says, "I'm sure your wife is in Heaven, getting a fantastic massage," because, even I can admit, that sounds weird.

The point is, those people who are saying things you don't like are still trying their best to help. And that's a good thing. So at the very least, accept that every wishful statement like that is an act of kindness.

And speaking of statements:

5. ALWAYS TELL THE PEOPLE YOU LOVE THAT YOU LOVE THEM.

This is something you have to do *before* the ones you love are gone. It's a tradition in my family, dating back to my father's childhood.

The story goes that he was with his cousin Myles, and Myles always told his father that he loved him. So my father asked why he did this, and Myles replied that he never knew if it would be the last time he saw his father.

So my father started always telling his parents that he loved them. And the tradition got passed down. In my family, we always finish conversations and phone calls by saying that we love each other. For a long time, the slightly morbid reasons for this were forgotten. We just did it.

And then my wife died.

But I knew that the last thing I had ever said to her was "I love you." It was also the last thing the kids had said to her—and the last thing she had told them. Which actually helped us to get through our grief.

Because there is nothing worse than thinking that someone died without you ever telling them that you loved them. After all, saying those three words is not a very hard thing to do. It takes no physical effort at all. But it means the world to people.

We have now arrived at my final piece of advice, which may also be the most unusual:

6. DON'T BE AFRAID TO LAUGH.

When you're grieving, you might feel that it's wrong to experience any joy at all, that everyone expects you to just be sad all the time. But think about that. Would the person who just died want you to be sad all the time? Would they even want you to be sad for just a few weeks? Or even a few days? I'm guessing the answer is no.

That doesn't mean that you *shouldn't* be sad. You should. If you're suffering from grief, it is totally okay to cry or mope or sulk or spend long periods of time in bed. But you can also cut yourself some slack. You can swap jokes with your friends. You can tell funny stories about the person who died. And you can even allow yourself some fun.

Remember, back at the beginning of this essay, when I said that there would be a happy ending? Well, here it is: the night of my wife's funeral, her wake turned into a dance party.

This was not planned.

Here's what happened: I was talking to my wife's best friend (who, to protect her reputation, I will call Patsy). My wife had always told me that when she and Patsy were younger and they might have had too much to drink, Patsy would occasionally insist on dancing like Bob Fosse (who was a famous choreographer). My wife thought

Patsy was not very good at dancing like this and always found it kind of embarrassing. But I had never seen Patsy's dancing.

And that night, Patsy started telling me about how my wife had always *loved* when they danced like Bob Fosse. Which was wrong, of course. My wife had obviously lied to Patsy about enjoying it so as to not hurt Patsy's feelings. But I wasn't about to tell Patsy that. Instead, I seized upon the opportunity to finally see Patsy dance. So I put on some Bob Fosse music (for the record, it was "All That Jazz" from *Chicago*). And Patsy danced.

I don't really remember if her dancing was any good or not. Because a curious thing happened. Other people started dancing, too. I always have a dance mix ready to go on my phone, so I started playing it, and pretty soon, *everyone* was dancing. And as we danced, we realized that this wasn't disrespectful at all. In fact, it was probably exactly what my wife would have wanted us to do.

It ended up being a very good dance party. People danced on the furniture. (I know your parents don't like when you do this, but there are exceptions to every rule.) There were conga lines. There was really bad disco. And for a while, everyone was happy. That didn't mean we didn't still feel sad on the inside, but for a little while, at least, there was light in the darkness.

I realize that isn't exactly an "and we all lived happily ever after" ending. Honestly, my kids and I haven't reached that point yet. At this writing, it is not quite three years since my wife died, and we are still dealing with it. Our lives have gone on. We still miss her. We still have bad days. But we have good days, too. Days of hope and laughter and joy.

There is no quick and easy way past grief. It takes time and work and good friends. But you can get through it.

And it couldn't hurt to always have a dance mix ready to go on your phone.

STUART GIBBS is the author of four *New York Times* bestselling series—Spy School, FunJungle, Moon Base Alpha, and Charlie Thorne—as well as the new Once Upon a Tim series. He has also written for movies and television—and he has researched capybaras. Really. You can learn more about what he's up to at www.stuartgibbs.com.

THE ADVENTURES OF ME AND SUPERSQUIRT

by Sarah Mlynowski

When I was a kid, there was nothing I wanted more than a baby sister.
Nothing. Well, maybe a Malibu Barbie Dreamhouse, but my parents
had given me a quick "Too expensive" on that one.

But a baby sister! That was the dream. And finally, finally, when
I was six and a half, my dream came true. My mother was pregnant.
And she was going to have a baby girl at the end of August! But
then—surprise!—the baby came ten weeks early, in June. I was so
excited! Since my sister was a preemie, she was small—she weighed
only three pounds, two ounces, less than most of my dolls. My parents named her Aviva June, but for some unknown reason I decided
to call her the Squirt.

Aviva had to stay in the hospital for six weeks, the longest six
weeks of all time. I visited every day after school. Even though she
had a feeding tube coming out of her nose, I was allowed to carefully
hold her if I wore a white gown over my clothes to protect her from
my kindergarten germs. I whispered to her, again and again, "I love
you just because you're mine."

When she was finally allowed to come home, she was healthy

and tiny. I couldn't believe my luck—not only did I have my own living, breathing doll but also, I had a live-in best friend. By the time she was two, she had corkscrew curls, a devilish smile, and a constant desire to climb the furniture. I dressed her up in superhero costumes and did photoshoots. We built pillow forts. We made up games like Roller Coaster, where I would lift her and swing her around on my legs for hours, straight to the moon and back. I learned how to make French braids and did her hair. When I got a new art set, I shared it.

When I got the chicken pox, I shared it, too.

Being a good big sister wasn't my only childhood hobby. I was also an excellent worrier.

I spent a lot of time agonizing about all the terrible things that could happen: What if my teachers made me talk in front of the whole class and I forgot what I was supposed to say? What if I had to talk to a stranger and they thought I was weird? What if I rode a bike and got hit by a car? What if my parents got divorced? What if my house burned down? What if there was a green monster who lived under my bed and he pulled out my teeth while I was sleeping?

I had a bit of an overactive imagination. Luckily, my other favorite hobby was writing stories.

The Squirt became the star of them all.

I wrote *The Squirt, The Adventures of Supersquirt*, and *The Amazing Supersquirt Strikes Back*. They were all about a girl (Sarah) who had a younger sister (Squirt). Sarah and Squirt lived in Montreal, just like I did. Like the real Squirt, this Squirt loved to climb furniture and jump. Plus she could fly. The real Squirt had another kind of magical power—unlike me, she was fearless. She didn't just talk in public, she *sang* in public, she learned to ride a bike at three, plus she talked to everyone. I was a bit jealous, but mostly I was proud. She was amazing, and she was mine.

Despite the seven-year (okay, Aviva, six-and-a-half-year) age difference, my sister and I really were best friends.

And I was happy. My sister was happy.

Apparently, my parents were not that happy.

And then there was a plot twist.

The day after my twelfth birthday, my parents told me and Aviva to come sit at the kitchen table because they had something to tell us. My dad took a deep breath and my mother bit her nails. They hesitated.

I suddenly knew what was coming. *Divorce.* It was what I had been worrying about! My worries had come true! I started crying before they said the word.

Aviva, who was only five, got scared. "Sarah is crying for no reason!"

Which made me cry even harder. My sister had no idea what was coming, and I wanted to wrap my arms around her and shield her from finding out. I wanted to protect her.

My mother turned to her. "Daddy's not going to live here anymore."

Even when my parents explained, Aviva still didn't really understand what was going on, but then she started crying, too. I couldn't stop. I'd been right to worry. Bad things happened, and there was nothing I could do to stop them.

I hugged my sister and didn't want to let go. I couldn't keep my parents from getting divorced, and I couldn't protect her.

Custody arrangements were made. My dad moved out. We lived with my mom, but every second weekend my dad would pick us up and drive us to his new apartment. We shared a room there, and when I couldn't fall asleep, I'd listen to her soft breathing and let it lull me to sleep.

That next year was hard. My dad took Aviva and me all the way from Montreal to Disney World, trying to cheer us up. While everyone else at the park seemed to be having the time of their lives, I was drowning. I was strapped into the ride of Spaceship Earth, feeling like the world was too big, I was too small, and what was the point of anything?

As the days passed, and shuttling back and forth between my parents became the new normal, I started to find my balance again. I started middle school. I loved my classes. I found a crew of friends: Mel! Shobie! Judy! I had a boyfriend. I was happy again. A scary thing had happened, but I was okay.

And there was another plot twist.

When I started ninth grade, my mom met a new guy at work. He was a consultant from Connecticut. Before their first date, my mom joked, "Maybe we'll get married and we'll all move to Connecticut."

"Fun," Aviva said. "What's Connecticut?"

"I'm not moving to Connecticut," I told them. "I'll finish high school with Daddy and then come for college."

"Won't you miss us?" my mom said.

"Yes," I said. "But I'm not moving."

They had a great date.

"I'm still not moving," I reminded her.

They fell in love.

"Not. Moving."

They got engaged.

"But moving would be so exciting!" my mom said. "A new city! A new house! New friends!"

I liked my old friends just fine, thank you very much.

Their plan was to live in Connecticut for a few years but then move to Arizona.

"It's always sunny in Arizona," my mom said. "And warm! Don't you want to live somewhere warm?"

That day it was about minus fifty in Montreal. My eyelashes froze to my skin. When I exhaled, the cold air made it look like I was smoking.

But I did not want to leave my school. I did not want to leave Mel, Shobie, and Judy. I did not want to leave my boyfriend. I did not want to leave my dad. The very idea of starting over in a new school, a new city, a new country, filled me with worry and dread. It was the drowning feeling all over again. I could not handle any more change. It was too much. "I'm not moving," I insisted. "You can't make me move. I'm not starting over in Connecticut and then starting over in Arizona two years later. No way." Were they kidding me?

I knew I would miss my mother and my sister, but missing them seemed less terrifying than leaving everything else behind. Aviva would be fine! She was brave! She would make lots of new friends. "I'll visit all the time," I told her. "And I'll go to college in Arizona. So we'll be back together eventually. Everything will be fine! Totally fine!"

"Okay," she said, hugging me. She trusted me.

Maybe my parents agreed to the new plan because they thought staying would make me happier. Maybe they agreed to it because it made the custody arrangements easier. Maybe because it was easier to lose one of us than both of us. I think it was a little of all three. But it was decided: I would move in with my dad and stepmother. My sister would move to Connecticut with my mom and her new husband. We were living a real-life version of *The Parent Trap*.

As the moving day got closer, I started picking fights with my mother and arguing with my sister. I spent as little time with them as possible.

I wanted to make it hurt less.

While my mom packed up and sold the house we had grown up in, Aviva and I went to sleepaway camp.

All summer I told myself—it's going to be fine!

Totally fine!

On our last night together, my sister and I broke down. Tears streamed down our faces. What had I done? Aviva was only nine! She was going to grow up without me! She would get too big for Roller Coaster! Who would teach her all the things a big sister should? Like how to deal with friend drama and scary teachers? Who would protect her? How could I let her down like this? I felt guilty and terrified and gutted all at once. But I couldn't move. I just couldn't.

"I love you all the time. Just because you're mine," we told each other, through sobs.

The next morning, my dad picked me up from the camp bus and drove me to his house. My mom picked up my sister and they drove to the airport.

Over the next few years, I'd visit Connecticut every few months. Aviva would visit Montreal. We would talk on the phone every few days. We'd meet up every summer at sleepaway camp.

But then my mom and stepdad decided to really move to Arizona—which was even farther from Montreal and in a different time zone. We missed each other's calls. Finding time to spend together became harder. I wanted to travel instead of going to camp. I decided to stay in Montreal for college. My dad and stepmom moved to Toronto, so when Aviva visited them, I wasn't always around. When I visited my mom, Aviva had made her own friends, and she had her own life going on. Getting time together was harder.

Eventually, I became a novelist in New York. Aviva ended up a reality TV producer in Los Angeles. I got married and had two kids. Twenty-five years later, we were no longer in separate countries, but we were now on opposite coasts, still in different time zones, and we only saw each other a few times a year.

Our lives had gone in different directions. When I told people we were split up as kids, everyone always asked if we were close.

"So close," I'd say, because we still were. We talked and texted all the time. She was the maid of honor at my wedding. When she had meningitis and was in the hospital, I was on the first plane over. She was there for my daughters' birthdays. She brought them cool clothes. Much cooler clothes than I could have. She was still my best friend.

I still wrote about her, too. My first YA series was called Magic in Manhattan and was about a girl who finds out that her younger sister has magical powers. The big sister is a little bit jealous—but mostly proud. So basically, it was an updated version of Supersquirt.

The dedication says: "For Aviva, my baby sister. And yes, she'll always be my baby sister, even when she's seventy-two and I'm seventy-nine. (Fine, Aviva, seventy-eight and a half.)"

Aviva tells tells everyone that she's the star of all my books. And she is.

She's Miri from *Bras & Broomsticks*. Jonah from *Whatever After*. Devi in *Gimme a Call*. She's my star, my muse, my Squirt.

Love doesn't disappear just because you live in another city.

People move. Sometimes by choice, and sometimes not.

That doesn't change who they are. That doesn't change who they are to you.

Aviva was still mine.

Want to hear another plot twist?

Last September, my family decided that we needed a change. We packed up our stuff and moved to Los Angeles.

Yeah, change is hard. Change is scary. But turns out, it's also exciting. New house! New city! New friends!

When I got here, Aviva was waiting for us at our new house. She jumped on top of me as we got out of the car. We both cried. "I can't believe you live here!" she cheered. "I can't believe this is my life!"

So now, Aviva and I live in LA. My dad and stepmom just moved to Vancouver. My mom and stepdad live in Vegas. We might not all live in the same house, or even the same country, but for the first time in twenty years, we all live in the same time zone.

(Also, my house is about fifteen minutes from Malibu. So although I never got my Malibu Barbie Dreamhouse, I came pretty close.)

But the best part? My girls get to grow up with their amazing aunt Vivi only a short drive away. And she's great at French braids and making up dances.

Plus her Roller Coaster is out of this world.

SARAH MLYNOWSKI is the *New York Times* bestselling author of over forty novels, including the Whatever After series, the Magic in Manhattan series, and the Upside-Down Magic series, which she co-writes and which was adapted into a movie for the Disney Channel. Originally from Montreal, Sarah now lives in Los Angeles with her family. Visit Sarah online at SarahM.com and find her on Instagram, Facebook, and Twitter @SarahMlynowski.

PANIC! AT THE MOVIES

by Julie Buxbaum

*When I was in elementary school, everyone I knew was afraid of some-*thing. (Actually, come to think of it, that's still true. Shh, don't tell, because adults definitely don't want kids to know this, but grown-ups are afraid of lots of things.) My friends' fears, unlike mine, though, all seemed pretty "normal." My best friend hated lightning. On stormy nights, she'd be wide-eyed and terrified, and in the middle of the night, would crawl into her parents' bed. (I've always loved lightning and its ominous crackle. It's always felt like the opening of the best kind of story.) Another friend hated bugs and spiders, while I've never met a daddy longlegs I didn't like. (I once had an encounter with a black widow, and I didn't even break a sweat.) My brother hated small, tight spaces. (I'm not a fan, either, to tell you the truth.)

All of these phobias have names: astraphobia, arachnophobia/ entomophobia, claustrophobia.

As a kid, though, what I was most afraid of in the world did not have a name, at least not one I'd ever heard. Even worse, what scared me the most seemed to be what everyone else most loved. When I was twelve years old, the two things that filled me with an almost unbearable dread were slumber parties and going to the movies. Often, life would serve me the double whammy of both at once.

"Oh my god, for my birthday party we are all going to see *Weekend at Bernie's*, and then my mom said we can sleep in the basement!" my best friend, Halee (still my best friend now, actually, thirty-one years later), reported gleefully over our peanut-butter-and-jelly sandwiches in the cafeteria at lunchtime.

"Great!" I said, while my stomach pretzeled into knots. I put my sandwich down, no longer hungry.

"Maybe we can play a trick on the first person to fall asleep? Like put their hand in water to see if they pee their pants?" another friend asked, laughing. I nodded, forcing my face to smile. No way would I be the first one to fall asleep, so worrying about wetting my sleeping bag was the least of my problems. I already knew I'd be awake all night.

A slumber party. And a movie.

Kill. Me. Now.

"I'll just have to make sure I can come. I need to ask my mom," I said, trying to find a way out of the situation. Maybe miraculously we'd already have plans to visit my grandparents. Maybe the earth would open up and swallow me whole. That seemed preferable to a movie *and* slumber party.

"It's my birthday! You're my best friend. Of course you have to come!" Halee said. She was right. I considered myself a good best friend—we even had matching half-heart BEST FRIENDS FOREVER necklaces slung around our necks to prove it—and good best friends don't miss their best friend's birthday because they have completely irrational and secret fears. They just get over themselves. Right?

I don't remember the first time I found myself panicking during a movie. I suspect it was during *The NeverEnding Story*, because I remember that film as, well, never ending. Instead, most of the movie experiences of my childhood blur together. Like slumber parties, they were treated with the expectation that I would be excited, that they were a big treat. And I understood why. Tickets weren't cheap. I loved the buckets of buttery popcorn. I could even see the appeal of the dimming lights and the booming intro music.

But what I hated more than anything was what happened to me after. Because invariably, about thirty minutes into the film, my mind would begin to wander. My thoughts would stray from the story playing out on-screen to some other story playing out in my own mind. At the time, I didn't understand that this would one day turn into a sort of gift—my imagination's ability to run wild and out of control would be the foundation of my later life as a novelist.

But at the age of twelve, that distraction soon turned terrifying. It felt like the opposite of a gift. It felt like a sucker punch. Or falling down an endless hole of spiraling thoughts.

I was stuck in my seat in the theater. With at least an hour to go before the lights came up again. There was no escape from my own brain. Nothing could be scarier to me.

Here's how it would go down. On-screen, Johnny would be yelling, "Nobody puts Baby in a corner!" (If you don't get the reference, ask a parent. It's an iconic line from *Dirty Dancing*, a classic I've come to appreciate in more recent years.) In my head, a totally different scene would be playing out. I'd be overcome with dread and fear, a feeling so overwhelming I worried I might pass out.

I'd sit in my seat, hands grabbing the armrests. I'd curl my toes in my shoes to keep myself steady. I'd begin to sweat. My chest would hurt, like someone was hollowing out a space in the center of my lungs. My breaths would come quickly, and I'd try to steady the shaking. The feeling had happened enough times that I came to understand that I wasn't sick. It wasn't that I had eaten too much popcorn, or had skipped lunch, or was about to get the flu. The feeling was pure fear, similar to the feeling I'd get when jumping off a high diving board, but 1,000 percent worse, because there was no thrill attached—and worse yet, no bragging rights.

Everyone else had no problem watching *Honey, I Shrunk the Kids* or, most embarrassing of all, *The Little Mermaid*. I never told my parents. Or Halee. Never once said, "Hey, let's not go to the movies." Never once let them know about the way my stomach would fall, my brain would whirr, how sometimes I thought I might die if the movie didn't end soon.

Even now, I am not sure why I suffered in silence. Maybe because it was just too weird. Just too embarrassing. Just too . . . irrational.

I was afraid of what, exactly? Of movies? No, that wasn't it. I was afraid of getting distracted from the movie, and the torture my brain would offer when that happened—my own spinning out while everyone else sat engrossed and happy. How do you explain such complicated feelings when you haven't yet developed the vocabulary? No one had given twelve-year-old me the words.

I have the words now. Two of them, actually. And it wasn't until adulthood that I was able to identify what used to happen to me in the darkness of those theaters. I would have what a psychologist would call a "panic attack."

If you haven't had a panic attack, the Mayo Clinic's website describes it as a sudden bout of intense fear that can trigger a response in your body. Twelve-year-old me would describe it as an unexplainable downward spiral of dread and loneliness that would leave me drenched in sweat and panting. It came on without warning and without a real reason. Like a monster waiting for the end of act one on-screen to pounce on me in my seat.

Of course, the same thing would happen to me at slumber parties. At Halee's birthday party, slowly, one by one, the girls around me would slip into sleep, and Halee's basement would turn into a chorus of snoring. I'd lie awake, looking around in wonder at everyone else. It felt like their ability to fall asleep somewhere new was a superpower I didn't possess.

Instead, I was like the princess in "The Princess and the Pea." The floor was hard. The sleeping bag did not smell like my comforter at home, did not drape across my shoulder with the same amount of weight. The house was too hot or too cold and definitely too loud. Clearly some of these girls should possibly see a doctor about their sinus problems. That amount of snoring couldn't be healthy.

I'd try to remain brave. So what that I couldn't sleep? There were worse things than sitting up through the night. It's not like there were *actual* monsters here. And it's not like anything bad would happen if I watched my friends snore. Tomorrow I'd be tired and probably a little cranky. Sleep wasn't important, I told myself, though of course, I knew that sleep *was* important. My parents had drilled into me how necessary it was that I get a good night's rest, that my brain development depended on it.

While I lay there in the dark, I thought about how I was damaging my already clearly damaged brain. I felt the now familiar tornado of panic rear up. What was wrong with me?

Again, I didn't have the words.

I don't know what would have happened had someone explained to twelve-year-old me that I was suffering from "panic attacks."

That my frequent bouts of nervousness, not just during movies and sleepovers but also at the lunch table with friends, even at night in the comfort of my own perfect, pea-free bed, also had a name: anxiety. That what I was feeling was not something embarrassing or weird or any different from anyone else's fears—though mine, of course, were turned up a notch.

I don't think knowing what they were would have solved my problem entirely, but it definitely would have made the experience a whole lot less lonely. Tons of people have panic attacks. Tons of people have anxiety. Tons of people are scared of all sorts of random things.

Did you know there is something called phobophobia? It's a fear of *having* a phobia! There's also hexakosioihexekontahexaphobia, which is the fear of the number 666. I don't have either of those, but sometimes I wonder if I have nomophobia, the fear of not being able to use a mobile phone.

It's funny how naming something can take away much of its power. I don't have panic attacks anymore. I do still have anxiety. (I was about to write "suffer from anxiety" but then realized that's not quite true. I don't "suffer" so much from it anymore, mostly because I've asked for help and have found the tools to manage it.) I now love going to the movies, though I'm still not a huge fan of sleepovers. (The floor is still too hard. Halee's basement is still too noisy.)

I can name my fears. I can even write them down right here for you to read without shame or embarrassment. Twelve-year-old me didn't have a damaged brain, only an overly imaginative and sensitive one. So if I could go back in time, these are the words I'd hand myself, when I was gripping on to the movie seat armrests for dear life, another kind of gift: *panic attack*, *anxiety*, and most important, *hope.* I watched *The Little Mermaid* not too long ago with my own children. When I got bored thirty minutes in, I let my mind wander and relished the time to explore my own imagination. It wasn't scary there at all.

JULIE BUXBAUM is a *New York Times* bestselling author of novels for kids, teens, and adults. She's the author of *The Area 51 Files*, her debut novel for middle grade readers; five young adult novels (*Tell Me Three Things*, *What to Say Next*, *Hope and Other Punch Lines*, *Admission*, and *Year on Fire*); and two novels for adults (*The Opposite of Love* and *After You*). She is a former lawyer and graduate of Harvard Law School and lives in Los Angeles with her husband, two children, and more books than is reasonable. Visit Julie online at JulieBuxbaum.com and follow her @JulieBuxbaum on Instagram.

WHAT'S IN A NAME?

by James Ponti

My name is James.

If I have the good fortune of meeting you face-to-face, please feel free to call me that. After all, if you've read my writing, then we're not really strangers anymore. We're just friends waiting to be introduced. However, if you're a young reader, I know you'll probably call me *James Ponti*, with both names scrunched together like they're one word.

I've learned this from countless school visits during which students almost always say things like "Hello, James Ponti," or "Come over here, James Ponti." This happens to many of my writer friends. Pam Ryan told me she's always addressed as "Hello, Pam Muñoz Ryan," with all three names, just like they are on the covers of her amazing books.

I think the book covers are the reason. If you call me James Ponti, then you're not only talking to me, you're talking to the books, too. That's the power of a name. It can change who we are, how we're perceived, and even the way we think about ourselves.

This is why I spend so much time coming up with the character names in my books. Each one has to feel right and help tell the story. I chose *Molly Bigelow* for the main character in *Dead City* because it had a built-in contradiction—*big* and *low*—that was ideal for her personality. I picked *Florian Bates* for *Framed!* because I wanted it to be as different and unique as he was.

But, in addition to the names inside my books, I also picked the one that goes on the covers. You see, I've always been James, but I haven't always been James Ponti. It's a name I selected for myself in middle school because I wanted to take control of my identity.

To understand what I mean, we have to go back to my very beginning. It's hard to explain because I don't know the truth about myself. Not the whole truth. And I've long accepted that I never will.

Here's what I do know. My mother was a painter and a teacher who was divorced and had two children, my brothers Carey and Terry. She went on a trip to Italy, met my father, fell in love, and decided to move the family there from Florida.

Whether she ever married my father or not is uncertain. From a legal standpoint, he couldn't marry my mother because he was already married to someone else. In Italy, at the time, it was illegal to get a divorce. This became a problem when I was born.

Since he couldn't legally be married to my mother, he couldn't be listed on my birth certificate. All that was written in the space where the father's name goes was the word *Unknown*. My baptism certificate is even more confusing, as I'm listed with three separate, complete names: one with my mother's maiden name, one with the last name of my mother's first husband, and one with the last name of my actual father. Each is separated by the letters *aka*, which stand for *also known as*. It reads like a police file with different aliases listed for a criminal. Except I wasn't a criminal. I was just a baby.

A year later, we moved back to the United States, and my father disappeared from our lives. I have a few photographs but absolutely no memory of him. My mother told my brothers and me that he died, but over the years I came to realize that he simply left us, and she didn't want to tell us the truth. It's a messy origin story, but it's the only one I have.

The name situation got even more confusing when my mother remarried and hers changed again. When I started elementary school, I went by *Ponti*, my brothers went by their father's last name, and my mother went by my stepfather's.

It was a lot to keep track of, and sometimes I went by my stepfather's name to make it easier for others, but this just caused more confusion. At the end of first grade, a meeting was called, and my mom came to school to talk to my teacher and one of the administrators. They all looked at me and said that I had to pick one and stick with it.

It was a big decision for a seven-year-old to make, and I didn't want to choose. I felt like if I changed my name, it would be disrespectful to my father and my past. But if I didn't, it might hurt the feelings of my stepfather. It would be as though I was rejecting him.

"How about if I switch every year?" I suggested. "I'll just be Ponti in the odd-numbered years."

The administrator laughed at this but said, "No, you have to pick one."

Also weighing on the decision was the fact that my stepfather had said that he was going to adopt me, which would legally change my name. That's how *Ponti* disappeared from my life at the end of first grade. I changed so that now my name matched my mother's and stepfather's.

I have nothing against my stepfather. I am grateful for much of what he did for our family. But the truth is, I don't have a lot of positive things to say about him. We were never a good fit. I wasn't interested in the things he wanted me to be interested in. I didn't like hunting or fishing. I wasn't mechanically minded or good at fixing things. Likewise, he had no interest in the things that I enjoyed, like school, sports, or writing.

He also had no interest in adopting me.

I kept waiting for it to happen, and it never did. I had picked his name because I didn't want him to feel rejected, and yet he rejected me. Much later in life, my mother explained that he'd told her that if he adopted me, then I might someday come after his money. This was telling, because it implied that he knew early on that he wasn't going to be a permanent part of the picture. It was also comical. Never in his life did he have any money to go after.

He left the summer before I started the eighth grade. He'd already met someone else and remarried soon after he divorced my mother. I think he probably did adopt that woman's children. I don't know for sure. I don't care in the least. Even though he still lived in the same relatively small community, I saw him only once or twice a year. The day he walked out the door, he walked out of my life in every way except one.

I was stuck with his name.

Eighth grade was not good. I was at my most awkward. My most lost. It was made worse by the financial worries at home. My brothers were in college, and my newly single mother was trying to support us by running a small business out of our house.

I could see the worry on her face every day, and I felt it in my heart.

At one point we had a school trip, and the day before we were supposed to go, my teacher pulled me aside. He wanted to know why I hadn't turned in my permission slip. It wasn't like me to skip such things.

I told him that I wasn't going. I hadn't told my mother about the trip because I didn't want her to worry about paying for it. It cost less than ten dollars, but that still seemed like a lot. When he told my mother, she explained that she could still afford things like that, but I was worried.

At the end of eighth grade, the assistant principal came up to me and asked if I'd thought about running for student council office for the next year. (When I was growing up, ninth grade was part of middle school, which was called junior high school.) I told her that I'd thought about it but didn't know what I could run for.

"How about president?" she asked.

I laughed. There was no way I could ever get elected to that. The president was always someone who was popular, and that was something I was not. Despite this, I decided to try. Because I wasn't well known, I gave a speech, meant to be humorous, during which I said my name more than twenty-five times. It got lots of laughs, and that alone made it worth it. Amazingly, the speech swung things my way, and I won the election.

This was a huge confidence boost going into ninth grade. I'd turned a corner and was slowly but surely finding my way. I played on the football team. (I was awful.) I played on the basketball team. (I was not good, but not awful.) I improved as a student. I was happy and looking forward to going to high school and making a name for myself.

A name.

At the end of ninth grade, there was to be a big awards ceremony, and I thought I might actually win an award or two. It felt good, especially considering how rocky things had felt during eighth grade. But then I had a troubling thought.

My town had a weekly newspaper that reported on everything at the local schools. If I won something, it would be listed. And while most kids wanted their name in the paper, I didn't. Because it wasn't my name. It was my stepfather's. My *former* stepfather's.

I imagined the people who worked with him seeing that—his name—in the paper and congratulating him at work. They wouldn't know that he had absolutely nothing to do with me. They wouldn't know that he had nothing to do with any achievement or accomplishment that I made.

It didn't seem right. I wasn't angry at him, but I definitely didn't want him to get credit for anything to do with me.

And that's when I decided to take charge of my identity. I didn't talk to my mother or ask permission. I didn't discuss it with my brothers or my friends. I just walked into the principal's office and told him that there was something important we needed to discuss. He thought I was there because of student council and the end of the school year, so we sat at his desk.

My mind shot back to the end of first grade eight years earlier. I'd made the decision once. I could make it again.

"Mr. Davis," I said. "If you open my school records, you will see that my legal name is James Ponti. That's what I want to be called from now on. I don't ever want to hear that other name again."

He looked at me and could tell that I was serious. I don't know if he called my mother after. But then, while we were together in his office, he just nodded and said, "Okay."

And that was it.

At some point that day, the weight of what I'd done occurred to me. Whatever the truth was about my father didn't matter; that was back in Italy. And whatever my stepfather did or didn't do didn't matter, because I no longer had any connection to him. My brothers had a different last name, and my mother had a different last name.

I was the only Ponti.

This didn't make me feel lonely. I felt strong. I felt empowered. I had a total reset in life. There was no history or reputation or baggage to deal with. Whatever anyone thought of my name, good or bad, would be my doing. I promised myself that day I wouldn't do anything to hurt it. I would make sure it was never something my children would be embarrassed by.

I was still awkward and geeky and all sorts of things. But I owned my identity and was free to make it whatever I wanted.

My name is James.

You can call me that. But if you know me from my books and feel better calling me James Ponti, I'm cool with that, too. For you, it's a name that evokes stories about underage spies and teen detectives. For me, it's a name that tells the story of a middle schooler trying to figure out how he fits into the world.

A kid just like you.

JAMES PONTI is the *New York Times* bestselling author of three middle grade book series: City Spies, about an unlikely squad of five kids from around the world who form an elite MI6 spy team; the Edgar Award–winning Framed! series, about a pair of tweens who solve mysteries in Washington, DC; and the Dead City trilogy, about a secret society that polices the undead living beneath Manhattan. He lives with his family in Orlando, Florida. Find out more at JamesPonti.com.

COLORS OF JUNE

by Rex Ogle

Out of nowhere, a couple of jerk seventh graders start pushing me around in the gym locker room, making fun, calling me names. Usually, I just go with it. But today? Today, for some reason, I've had enough. I can't take it anymore. So I take a swing—and miss. They shove me into the lockers, and my own face runs into my own stupid hand. Everyone gets a good laugh at that.

"Dummy hit himself!"

"Gave himself a bloody nose!"

"What a moron."

This real bright red spills all over, down my bare chest. I walk over to the sink to clean myself off. I have to stick paper towels up my nose. More snickering from the jerks behind me. I wait till the gushing stops to finish changing into my PE uniform. That's why I'm late to gym class. But the coach is all "Detention! You know the rules." I try to explain, but he just blows his whistle at me. Like he doesn't want to hear it. Like I'm the problem.

So now I'm walking home after school, my nose bleeding again for no reason, and my hand is all bright sticky red, and the sky is blue.

Walking home, I notice all the white bricks and black roof tiles of the government-subsidized housing. It reminds me of this black-and-white show I used to watch with my grandma June when I was little. It was called *Zorro*, and it was about this hero with a sword and a mask who rode a horse. I miss June. I miss how easy life was when I was six or seven and all I cared about were toys and candy and snuggling with my grandma on the couch watching TV.

Now all I think about is how much I hate bullies, and stupid gym coaches, and how Mom is gonna flip when she sees I got detention. Again.

It's not even like I can forge her signature. I mean, I totally can. But detention is an hour after school, and I gotta be home so Mom can head to work at Bo Bo China. She waits tables, and she can't be late. So me getting detention means she has to stay home with my brother for another hour, and that means she makes less money, and that's all my fault, too.

Everything is my fault.

I hate it. I hate it and I wish I could just fly away. Off into the blue sky. Blue feels like freedom. And now I'm angry 'cause I have to go inside, inside our dark, crappy apartment, and take care of my brother and do my homework and make dinner and clean the house before my stepdad comes home. 'Cause if he comes home and dinner's not ready, I'm done for.

So yeah. That's all the stuff I'm thinking about when I walk inside my apartment, so I'm in a real crummy mood. I throw my backpack on the floor and kick off my shoes, all dramatic-like. My little brother, Shelby, is watching cartoons, eating Goldfish crackers, making me wish I didn't have to go to school, either.

Mom is ironing her waitress apron, only she's in a different mood. Different 'cause usually she's either real happy or real angry. There's no real in-between with her. Happy or angry. Usually. But today, she's different. Today, she puts down the iron, steam rolling up with a hiss, and looks at me, like she feels real bad for me.

Like she knows about the bullies and, for once, is gonna take my side.

But she doesn't know. Does she?

Then she sits down on the couch and pats the cushion next to her. "Come sit down with me."

"Why?" I ask, like it's some kinda trick.

She says, "Please." Now I'm worried.

"What's wrong?" I ask.

"I have some bad news." Mom is staring at her hands. They're all gnarled from washing dishes too much. They look like vulture talons, all old, even though Mom's face is real young. But right now, her eyes are all sad. She says, "Your father called." Usually that's bad. Mom and Dad don't like each other since the divorce. But again, she's not angry. She's sad. Mom tries to take my hand. "Your dad's mother—your grandma June—she has cancer."

The whole day runs through my mind. Tripping in front of my crush, Amber. Failing a science quiz and realizing I'm gonna have to do a bunch of extra credit to make up for it. Then the locker room situation: the push, me punching myself, the blood, detention. The way Mom is gonna flip out when I tell her, and shout at me, saying, "We're already behind on bills, Rex! Every time you get detention, that's money out of my pocket!"

The whole world suddenly feels all heavy, like it weighs a million tons. Like elephants and whales and dinosaurs are all stacked on my chest, so heavy that I can't breathe. And I'm so angry, 'cause there's nothing I can do except take whatever life dishes out at me . . .

That's when I shout, "Yeah, well, that's what she gets! What'd Grandma June expect when she smokes a pack a day?"

Mom slaps me.

Not hard. Not like when she's real angry. But enough to wake me up.

"It's not lung cancer," she says all soft. "It's breast cancer."

That's when I start crying. Like real hard crying. Sobbing. 'Cause I really love my grandma June. I only see her like once a year since the divorce, but on my dad's side of the family, she's the only one who loves me for real. She calls from Tennessee just to say hi and writes me letters for my birthday and Christmas. And when I visit, she always sneaks me a bag of chocolate-covered pretzels 'cause she knows how much I like them. She doesn't even make me share with my cousin.

I love Grandma June so much, and I know that cancer means she's probably gonna die, and all these tears are coming out of me, because I can't take back what I just said. I said it, and now it's out there, in the air, in the universe, and if she dies—

"I take it back," I cry, "I take it back. I didn't mean what I said. I didn't mean it! I don't want her to die. I don't."

Mom kneels down and wraps her arms around me.

She holds me for a real long time while I cry.

When I call her, Grandma June says, "How ya doing, Bubba?" Rex is my real name, but Rex is also the name of my dad and his dad, too. That makes me the third Rex in our family, Rex the Third. But in Tennessee, my grandpa is the only Rex. That makes my dad Buster, and my name turns into Bubba. I hate when anybody calls me

Bubba—except Grandma June. I don't mind when she says it 'cause she says it with a smile.

"I'm okay. How are you doing?"

"I'm well enough. The Lord will take care of me."

"How's the—the—" No matter how hard I try, I can't say the c-word. Cancer.

"Let's not talk about that," Grandma June says. "Tell me how school's going."

We're talking about dumb stuff like my grades and the weather in Texas and what I want for Christmas. But all I can think about is June's too-soft skin and her curled hair that spends hours in rollers getting just right and her big glasses like they wore in the seventies. I think about the way she'd sort her playing cards, moving them one by one, while playing gin rummy with the other adults, careful not to let anyone see her cards—then she'd peek over the top, at me across the room, and wink.

I'm thinking about all the happy times, and I feel this big ache spring up in my chest, 'cause I live in Texas and Grandma June lives in Tennessee and even though it's close on a US map, it's not really all that close in real life. It's far away. And I can't see her. And I want her to hold on until I can. I want her to stick around until I'm older. Till I finish up middle school, till I graduate from high school, and college, and get my first job. I want her at my wedding, I want her to hold my baby. Maybe I'll have a son, and I'll name him Rex, too, and I'll let her come up with the nickname. Not Buster or Bubba, but maybe Beau or Brody or Boudreaux. Something with a *B*. Or we'll just call him Rex the Fourth.

All I want is for her to get better. She has to, right? She's stronger than this. And I want to believe that. And I do.

Until I hear the wheeze in her voice. Like the woman who used to give me piggyback rides and carry me on her shoulders on hikes through the Smoky Mountains can't quite hold up the phone without losing her breath.

She says, "I need to go, sweetie, I'm a little tired."

I say, "I love you."

And she says, "I love you, too, Bubba. You're always in my prayers."

Now, every time I get off the phone with her, I wonder if it'll be the last time I hear her voice.

I usually visit my dad once a year. Sometimes for Christmas, sometimes for summer. This year, I'm doing summer. He, my stepmom, and my stepsister live on an air force base in Oklahoma right now. It's all hot, and everything is yellow. The sun, the commissary, the dead grass, the fence around the base swimming pool. Yellow and dusty.

My dad's house is a whole lot nicer than the apartment I live in with my mom, but I'd still rather be in Texas. My stepmom makes us kids clean every day. My stepsister dusts and I vacuum, and the vacuum is practically a tank, it's so big, and every time I bump into the wall or a corner or a piece of furniture, Nora shouts, "Careful!"

But the thing that really drives me nuts is this calendar on the wall in the kitchen. It's all pictures of kittens, which is cute, I guess, but every time I walk past, I'm looking at this month, the month of June. June, like my grandma. My dad's mom.

At the end of the month, we're supposed to go visit Tennessee, for the Fourth of July. We're gonna go see fireworks in Gatlinburg. I'm annoyed we have to wait so long.

Grandma June's still sick. It's been months and months and months. I keep thinking she'll get better. Believing she's got to. And I do most of the time, at least till the times when Dad gets off the phone with my aunt Debbie and he's got this faraway look in his eyes. Like he's left his body. Like he's way off on Pluto or something, and he's so cold and alone and . . .

Scared.

His face looks the way I feel on the inside.

I hate it. And I hate that the calendar keeps reminding me every time I go to get a glass of water. Or milk for my cereal. Or sandwich stuff. Or when I'm helping make dinner. It's like the calendar is always right there, reminding me June is sick, when all I wanna think about is her getting better. She has to get better. She has to . . . right? I want her to get better. She's my grandma. And I love her. And I don't want her to go away.

I know what happens when people die.

They don't come back.

And I can't even think about that. Not even a little.

"Wake up," Dad says. His hand is on my chest, shaking me awake.

I sit up in the darkness, freaked out. "Is the house on fire?"

"What? No." But then his lip trembles. Like he might break if he says anything else. So he doesn't. Instead, he gets up and leaves the room.

The hall light comes on, I hear footsteps and whispers. Then a sniffle. Then my dad is crying real hard. And I feel sick 'cause I've never heard my dad cry. I didn't even know he could.

Then Nora comes in my room. She sits on my bed. Even though she's close, she seems real far away. I ask, "What is it?"

She rubs my arm gently. "Grandma June took a turn for the worse. We're going to see her. We're driving to Tennessee. We're leaving tonight. Now, actually. Get dressed."

The world is pitch-black, the night sky weighing heavy on it like a wool blanket. I lean my head back, over the headrest, staring up and out the rear window, craning my neck to see the stars. There's no moon.

I think of Grandma June. Of the way she smiles.

I think of her basement closet, a collection of mason jars filled with fruits and vegetables, every one she canned herself. Sometimes I'd help her shuck the yellow cobs of corn, or pull the orange carrots from below the surface of brown dirt, or pluck the tender red tomatoes, which I refused to eat. I think of summer days, when we'd pick from among the green vines, first raspberries, then blackberries, each staining my little hands in specks and ribbons of sticky scarlet or black-blue. For every two I'd pick, I'd eat one and giggle. June's lips would curl up at the corners, and she'd say, "Save me some if you want me to make you a pie."

I think of the little gold chain that hung from her glasses, around her neck, as if she were worried the glasses would leap from her face and run away. I think of her staying up, reading me church stories from a children's book that she bought for me. One story is about Noah's ark, with pairs of every kind of animal on a single boat, riding through a storm. Another is David and Goliath, making me wish I were good enough with a slingshot to take down a giant. And I think of Sundays at church with June, her dressed up in her best blue dress but squeezing my hand when I giggled during sermons. I think of a gift she gave me—a porcelain boy, in pastel-blue pajamas, on his knees, eyes closed, his hands in prayer.

I think of the dark purple nights, just after the sun had set, when fireflies would come out. I'd chase them until I caught one, cupping my hand oh so gently so that I could watch it up close, its tiny legs and feet crawling up my arm, its rump lighting up with a green-yellow glow—otherworldly—like some alien pet that I was the first to discover. Then we'd go inside to watch black-and-white movies on the TV. Grandpa Rex, the first Rex, would huff, wanting to watch a war movie, but June would shake her head, saying, "Bubba gets to pick tonight." I'd pick cowboys or something with aliens and space-ships, 'cause those were my favorite.

Thinking of her, so many memories of her, my eyes drift closed . . .

. . . until I fall asleep.

In my dream, June appears in an all-white place, wearing all white. She looks so young and strong. Without asking, I already know her pain is finally gone.

I run to her, and she hugs me for a long time. She whispers in my ear, but no words come out. But she's smiling.

I start crying.

And I wake up crying in the back seat of my dad's car. Outside, the sky is gray and raining, as if the world is crying with me.

By the time we get to Tennessee, June is already gone. All my hope that I'd get to see her one more time rushes out of me. All I can think about is what I said when I learned she had cancer. A pit in my stomach opens up, tightens, like I swallowed a snake, a boa constrictor twisting and turning inside me.

The first day is all gray and dark. The next, the sun comes out as we pull up at the funeral home. There are so many people here, so many strangers. Most of them friends from my grandparents' church. My stepsister hugs me, and my stepmom keeps kissing my forehead, and I'm glad I'm not alone.

But then I find out I have to stand at the front, next to the coffin, with my dad and grandpa, the three Rexes, all of us in black suits. When people walk up to pay their respects to Grandma June, first they have to shake our hands. Ten people into the line, a man raises a hook at me. I'm startled by the metal prosthetic. I hop back, scared to touch it for a second. But I think of June and what she'd do. I shake his hand (well, his hook), and he says, "I am sorry for your loss." A few minutes later, another hook-handed man shows up. I shake his hand (hook), too. The third time it happens, the man has long black hair, like Captain Hook. I recall seeing *Peter Pan* with Grandma June, and her impression of the pirates singing. I have to bite my tongue so I don't laugh. Instead, a snort escapes me.

My dad shakes his head, saying, "Don't be rude. It's a logging town."

After the funeral, we head home. To the house filled with so many memories of June. Of her playing gin rummy, of the black-and-white movie marathons, of the chocolate-covered pretzels she'd sneak to me, saying, "Our little secret."

People bring dish after plate after pan of food. Fried chicken, country ham, fried catfish, mashed potatoes, grits, green bean casserole, cornbread, pecan pie. But I'm not hungry. The snake inside my stomach churns, coiling and uncoiling, wanting to burst out of me. Like I want to scream.

With all the people and all the food, the house fills up too fast. Hook hands and church hats and so many strangers surrounding me, talking to me, trying to make new memories in a house that I want to save only for her. For June.

It's too much. I can't breathe.

So I run outside and across the gravel road. To the edge of the hillside. And I do scream.

I scream and scream and scream.

Until I'm on my knees.

Crying.

Staring out at the sun setting over the Smoky Mountains. The most brilliant colors of tangerine and gold and amber and rose light up the sky in waves blurring into one another, the way I imagine the sun drops into the sea in Hawaii, setting the ocean on fire with a garden of brilliance.

It's the most beautiful sky I've ever seen. And Grandma June isn't here to share it with me.

Except that she is.

I can feel her. Not firm in reality, but surrounding me, as if on a breeze.

She's part of me now. She's in every raspberry I eat. Every haunted house I visit. Every firefly that walks on my arm. She's in every Dolly Parton song I hear. Every ashtray I turn my nose up at. In every black-and-white movie I watch. Every church hymn I hear. Every jarred peach I eat. Every piece of corn I get stuck in my teeth while gnawing on cobs. Every Christmas I share. Every chocolate-covered pretzel I sneak. Every card game I play. Every carrot I unbury. Grandma June is with me.

'Cause goodbye isn't really goodbye, not in my heart.

Before, Tennessee was far away from me. I had to wait for phone calls or letters or visits. But now my grandma June doesn't need a phone or a stamp or an airplane. She's here with me all the time.

On good days. On bad days. I'm never alone.

REX OGLE was born and raised (mostly) in Texas. He is the author of the memoirs *Free Lunch* (which received the YALSA Award for Excellence in Non-fiction) and *Punching Bag*, and the upcoming graphic novel *Four Eyes*. He also wrote the fantasy middle grade Supernatural Society trilogy and has written dozens of comics for Marvel and DC, as well as his webcomic, *Blink*.

He's written under a lot of pen names, too—most notably Trey King, Honest Lee, and Rey Terciero, under which he penned *Meg, Jo, Beth, and Amy* and *Swan Lake: Quest for the Kingdoms*.

Rex currently lives in Los Angeles. You can find out more about him and his stories at RexOgle.com or follow him on Instagram @ThirdRex, where he posts way too many pictures of his dog, Toby.

ON HOPES AND DREAMS

by Janae Marks

When I do author visits at schools and talk about my long road to getting a book published, a question kids often ask is, "How did you stay hopeful throughout your journey?" In other words, how did I keep writing throughout years of roadblocks and rejection?

Before I get into that, let me go way back to when I was a kid myself. Growing up, I didn't know that I wanted to become an author. But I loved books! I have vivid memories of spending time at my local library and borrowing books with my very own library card. I remember building my Baby-Sitters Club book collection, as it quickly became my favorite series. I even wrote the author, Ann M. Martin, a letter in elementary school. She mailed back what looked like a form letter, but it was still thrilling to receive something from my favorite author. (By the way, Baby-Sitters Club books are still around and have even been made into graphic novels!)

I also loved to write, though I wasn't writing entire novels back then. I started out writing short autobiographical stories in kindergarten that always began with, "One day a girl named Janae . . ." In the second grade, my teacher had us create a lot of our own illustrated books, and he'd laminate the covers. I was always super proud of those stories and still have them to this day. In middle school, I wrote long entries in diaries and journals, and I exchanged letters regularly with one of my camp friends. In high school, I wrote short stories that I'd submit to *Seventeen* magazine's teen writing contests. My work never made it into the magazine, and I got my first glimpses of rejection as a writer. But that rejection didn't hurt because I didn't want to be an author anyway. I was just writing for fun.

In high school, I wanted to be on Broadway. I was obsessed with musicals and singing, so my extracurricular activities were dance classes, acting classes, and voice lessons.

And here's where the hope starts to come in. Getting onto Broadway is very hard. Most kids who want to become Broadway performers when they grow up don't make it. But my parents, and especially my mom, encouraged me to go after it anyway. Why? Because when she was younger, my mom had her own dream. She dreamed of becoming a fashion designer. She always loved to sew and make her own clothes and thought that she could make a career out of it.

But her parents said no. It's not that they didn't think she had what it took, but they didn't think it was a practical career. You see, my mom had grown up poor in Harlem, New York. Her parents wanted the best for her, and for them, that meant finding a job that was more stable and provided consistent income. Without their support, my mom felt that she couldn't study fashion design in college. She majored in math instead. She went on to work for a computer company, and then became a math teacher after I was born. She never stopped sewing—trust me when I say that the Halloween costumes she sewed for me growing up were incredible! But she did not try to make a career out of it, as she'd always dreamed. She later told me that this was one of the biggest regrets of her life.

So, when I told her what my dream was, even if it wasn't super realistic, she supported it 100 percent. She felt happiness in one's career was more important than anything else. Because of this, she drove me to my classes and encouraged me every step of the way. That encouragement to go after my dreams gave me so much hope, even when things got hard. Like during my senior year of high school when I auditioned for four college theater programs—and was rejected from every single one of them.

That time, the rejection really hurt. If I wasn't good enough to get into a college theater program, then how would I make it onto Broadway? I ended up going to a liberal arts college with a strong theater department and auditioned for a musical during my first year on campus. And then I realized that not getting into a theater program was a blessing in disguise, because by the end of freshman year, I'd had an epiphany. I realized that I wasn't outgoing enough for theater. That maybe it was the stories that I was drawn to the most, not the performing. I was happy to keep doing plays as an extracurricular activity, but maybe Broadway wasn't for me after all.

Sometimes dreams change like that, in an instant. Sometimes you wake up and realize that this dream you've been holding on to isn't the right one. And that's okay!

When it was time for me to declare a major in college, I thought about how much I'd loved reading and writing all my life. How much joy I got from doing creative writing assignments in school or writing short stories for fun. I became an English major and didn't look back.

Now I'll jump ahead a little. After college, I started a job in book publishing and went to the New School to get my MFA in writing for children and young adults. All the while, my parents continued to encourage me. This time, it felt like I'd found my true calling.

When I graduated with my MFA, I was certain that I'd get a book deal soon after with my first manuscript. In fact, many alumni from my same program—Jenny Han, Coe Booth, Lisa Greenwald—published books soon after graduation. I believed I had what it took. I just needed to find a literary agent—a person to represent my books and connect me with a publisher.

I sent queries—what they call the emails you send to pitch your book for representation—to dozens of literary agents. Many of them requested to read the manuscript, and lots of them had complimentary things to say. But ultimately, every single one of them rejected me. At a certain point, I realized it was time to put that book aside.

That was a tough moment. It brought back memories of when I got rejected from the theater schools. What if this meant I wasn't good enough to be published, either?

But I remained hopeful for a few reasons. For one, I truly believed in my writing. And from reading about other authors' journeys to publication, I knew that most writers don't publish the very first book they write.

So, I wrote a second book, and then a third. But I was still no closer to being published. Meanwhile, many of the writer friends I'd made along the way were getting literary agents and book deals. My writing community used to be filled with fellow aspiring authors, but now many of them were publishing their books. I was super happy for them but felt even more behind.

Still, I didn't quit. I never stopped writing. Why? Because I loved it too much. This is how I knew how much I loved it: With theater, as soon as I faced big rejection, I realized that I wasn't willing to fight for that dream. But this one? I was going to fight for it.

How did I do that? Even after getting my MFA, and while working a full-time job, I did whatever I could to improve my writing. For years I went to writing conferences and read craft books plus any writing advice I could find from already published authors. I took every opportunity to get my work critiqued by other authors or publishing professionals. I revised my stories repeatedly. I knew if my writing was the absolute best it could be, I'd have a better chance of getting it published.

Along the way, I learned that the publishing world is subjective. Sometimes, what matters more than the quality of your writing is whether your book idea is marketable. I got a sense of that when many of the rejections I received for my first manuscript said that it was "too quiet." In other words, it wouldn't stand out among all the other children's books being published. So I tried to think bigger when it came to my book ideas. What was an idea that could really hook a literary agent, publisher—and reader?

Finally, I had an idea. It felt bigger and more unique than anything I'd written before. The hope inside me bloomed. *This could be it!* But first I had to write it. I wrote a first draft over a few months, and then revised it multiple times with the help of my critique partners. I gave it a title: *From the Desk of Zoe Washington*. Once it felt polished, I sent queries to literary agents. I also sent pages from the book to a writing contest for unpublished children's book writers that a friend recommended.

Dear reader, *From the Desk of Zoe Washington* won that contest!

It also attracted the attention of multiple literary agents who wanted to sign me, and ended up in a publisher's auction. That meant multiple publishing houses wanted to publish it, so I had the choice of who I wanted to work with. Somehow, I was now in the position to send rejections. (While it was great to have my pick of agents and publishers, I did not enjoy rejecting anyone!)

All my perseverance, that hard work over eight years, and those moments of finding renewed hope had paid off. I was finally going to be a published author, and I was so excited!

When you have a goal and hit a roadblock, think of it as an opportunity. Do you want to pick yourself back up and keep trying? If the answer is no—like it was for my Broadway aspirations—then it's okay to move on to something new. Dreams can be fluid like that.

But if there's still a part of you, even deep down inside, that really wants to see yourself reach that dream? To see your book on a bookstore shelf, or whatever it is that your heart is tugging you toward, *keep going*. Take a break if you need to, but get back to it and find ways to keep your hope alive.

Grow it with outside inspiration, like I did with writing conferences and craft books. Find your community—friends, family members, or teachers who can encourage you along the way, especially when it gets hard. Celebrate all the positive milestones, like completing a project or sending your work out to someone. Be your own biggest cheerleader and keep telling yourself that you can do this!

Because you can. You can turn your hopes and dreams into reality, too.

I believe in you.

JANAE MARKS is the critically acclaimed author of the middle grade novels *From the Desk of Zoe Washington* and *A Soft Place to Land*. She grew up in the New York City suburbs and now lives in Connecticut with her husband, daughter, and miniature schnauzer. She has an MFA in writing for children and young adults from the New School. Visit Janae online at JanaeMarks.com.

MAJOR MALFUNCTION

by Tom Angleberger

"What's your major malfunction?"

This was a popular catchphrase in the early 1980s.

Not as popular as "Gag me with a spoon" or anything, but you heard it a lot.

Or at least . . . little Tommy Angleberger seemed to hear it a lot.

I associate it most with the fifth and sixth grades.

That was not long after *Star Wars* came out. "Major malfunction" sort of gave you this picture of a broken robot clanking in circles, spewing smoke, with gears and springs popping out.

It really seemed to sum up how the other kids saw me: a mess; a weirdo; a dweeb; a chatterbox; a blabbermouth; a dork; a jerk; a walking, talking malfunction.

It was more than just an insult. It may have been a very real question: What is wrong with this kid?

Some teachers were asking the same thing but with other words.

•   •   •

Let's be honest . . . I did do some really weird stuff.

Meltdowns. Freak-outs. Sobbing. Tying a plastic Garfield to my hooded sweatshirt strings and swinging it around like a medieval battle-ax or something.

All on full display to my whole class.

Who can blame them for wondering?

Looking back, I can sort of sympathize with them. Especially with one girl, Katrina, who really seemed to hate me.

I can imagine her starting middle school and thinking that she was taking a big step toward adulthood. The silly days of elementary school were behind her, and she was growing up. Things were going to be different in middle school. She'd meet the kids who had come from the other elementary schools, and a new era in her life would begin. A more mature, more sophisticated era would begin.

And then in stumbles Tommy: a child.

A loud child.

A loud, messy, annoying child who always seemed to be in her way and on her nerves. *What is this, kindergarten?*

Can't that brat just shut up?

No, I couldn't shut up.

That's the major malfunction (or one of them).

I wanted to shut up. I would sort of pray for silence. My own silence.

Let me just go to school and just sit there and not say anything. Let me just not . . . malfunction.

That didn't work.

I couldn't stop talking. I couldn't stop having meltdowns. And I couldn't seem to start growing up.

What *was* my major malfunction?

Well, what if I didn't actually have a malfunction?

What if there was something different about me that wasn't broken?

In fact, what if there was something different about me that really worked?

There was, but I didn't find out about it for many years.

I was and am autistic.

It wasn't a word you heard very often back then. Not nearly as often as you heard *dweeb*, *dork*, and *major malfunction*.

And even when I first started learning about it, I didn't realize it meant me.

But finding out that I was on the autism spectrum was a wonderful thing. A whole lot of stuff started to make sense at last.

Why was I often the only person doing something? Or the only person *not* doing something?

Why couldn't I just fit in?

Because I literally didn't fit in with all those "functioning" people. The place I fit in was "on the spectrum." And once I knew who to look for, I realized I hadn't been the "only one." There are lots of us.

I am really proud to belong to this amazing group of people who are also "on the spectrum." We're so different, yet connected.

Plus the phrase "on the spectrum" is a hell of a lot better than "major malfunction."

What I don't like, however, is another phrase: "autism spectrum disorder."

Disorder sounds an awful lot like *malfunction*.

And it's not a malfunction.

Sometimes, I call it a superpower.

Think about those superhero origin stories, where the hero gets the powers but doesn't know how to use them yet. And they make a big mistake and knock over a building or laser-blast something expensive.

Well, I didn't knock over a building, just annoyed Katrina and a few hundred others for a few years. (Sorry!)

But once I finally got it all figured out, I stopped talking and started typing and drawing.

And out came books.

And people liked (some of) the books.

Maybe because the books were about a kid with a "major malfunction" that was really a superpower.

And maybe because a lot of the readers were kids that had the same superpower.

Let's be honest.

There are a lot of times when this "superpower" still looks an awful lot like a "major malfunction." There are still times when I should keep my mouth shut and just type it all up later.

But so many of my dreams have come true, from writing *Star Wars* books to marrying another writer and illustrator, Cece Bell.

In the end, it isn't really a malfunction *or* a superpower. It's just me. I'm not a broken robot or a superhero.

Just a human.

Just a confused kid who hadn't figured it all out yet—and is still working on it.

Katrina and those other kids (and some teachers) were right that something about me wasn't working "normally."

But I wasn't broken, and I'm glad I didn't get "fixed."

Sure, I might have needed some help understanding and dealing with all of it, but . . . doesn't everybody need a little help, whether it's from a book, a song, a friend, a teacher, a therapist, a patient pet, or maybe even a paper finger puppet? (Answer: yes.)

I'm not sure what kids say today instead of "major malfunction." But whatever they say, maybe they've said it to you.

I'm not going to tell you to ignore it. But I am going to tell you not to believe it.

And for goodness' sake, don't try to fix yourself! You might "fix" yourself so that you act more like them, and then where would we be? A world full of Katrinas yelling at each other? No thanks.

No, don't fix it. Don't fight it. Don't hide it. Just have a little faith in it.

Your own combination of malfunction and superpower may have felt clunky today, but it may be exactly what you need tomorrow.

TOM ANGLEBERGER is the author of *The Strange Case of Origami Yoda* and many other books for kids. In addition to being a weird kid, he was also a short kid. The second shortest, in fact. Which may explain why he likes Yoda so much.

HOPE I DON'T SEE A GHOST

by R.L. Stine

I'm not a hopeful person. I usually hope against *things.*

I hope it rains so I don't have to go to that picnic.

I hope my cousin calls to cancel our lunch so I can stay home and relax.

I hope no one sees me eating this entire carton of ice cream.

I admit it. These are not hopes I can write about that will inspire people. Talking about these hopes will not inspire people to have hope.

But wait. I have had a hope that might be interesting to some people. I write many stories about the supernatural. And so, a lot of people ask me this question: "Have you ever seen a ghost?"

I always answer, "No, I haven't. But I keep looking."

That answer may not be true.

I may have seen a ghost nine or ten years ago. I'll tell you the story, and you can decide.

My wife, Jane, and I have a summer house in Long Island, New York, near the ocean. Two houses down from us, a man named Kravitz lived by himself. I don't know how old Kravitz was, but he was very old.

We liked him a lot. We often invited him over for backyard bar-becues. He had been the business manager of a circus, and he had hundreds of interesting stories.

One summer afternoon, we heard that Kravitz had been sick for a while.

"He's all alone over there," Jane said. "I'm going to make him something for dinner, and you can take it over to him."

She made a pasta dish, broad noodles with meat and cheese, and she put it in a blue casserole dish. I carried the dish down the block to Kravitz's house and made my way to his kitchen door.

It was a sunny day but cool, with a steady wind off the ocean. Sunlight filled the back window so that I couldn't see inside the house.

I knocked on the door and waited. Silence inside. Kravitz didn't come to the door.

I knocked again. He didn't appear.

"Hey, Kravitz—are you in there?" I called. (Everyone called him Kravitz.)

I was about to try the front door when I realized the kitchen door was open a crack.

"Kravitz? Are you awake?"

I pushed open the door and stepped into the kitchen. It was warm in the house, stuffy, as if all the windows had been closed for a while. The kitchen was clean and bare. No sign that Kravitz had eaten breakfast.

I set the casserole dish down on the counter. "Kravitz? It's me," I called. "Are you okay?"

He appeared in the doorway. I almost gasped when I saw him. He wore a long gray nightshirt, and his face was as gray as the nightshirt. He had dark crevices under his eyes, which were only half-open. His lips were dark, almost blue, and his chin trembled as he started to speak.

"You woke me." His voice was a dry whisper, like the wind through dead leaves. "You woke me."

"Sorry," I said. I stared at the gray nightshirt, avoiding his face. "Kravitz, how do you feel?"

He coughed. "I need to sleep now."

"Yes. Good," I said. "Jane made you a casserole." I pointed to the blue dish on the counter. "When you feel like eating . . ."

"I'll sleep . . ." he said.

I started to the door. "If you need anything," I said, "just call. We're two minutes away."

He nodded. His eyes were nearly closed. His face suddenly appeared dark and light, like the surface of the moon.

"Enjoy the casserole," I said. "It's still warm, if you want to eat lunch."

He nodded again.

I turned and went back out the door. I walked home thinking about how sick Kravitz looked. Maybe sleep would help him. I wondered if he had a good doctor. I should have asked.

I told Jane how I awoke Kravitz and how sick he looked. "You should look in on him tomorrow morning," she said. "See if he feels any better and see if he enjoyed the casserole."

And that's just what I did.

The next morning was gray, with storm clouds hanging low in the sky. I walked to Kravitz's house and stopped before the driveway. There was a big truck, a moving van, beside the house. Workers were carrying an armchair to the truck.

I walked up the driveway and stopped one of the workers. He was a big, bearded man in denim overalls and a flannel shirt. "What's going on?" I asked him.

"You're a neighbor?" he said.

I nodded. "Yes."

"I guess you didn't hear," he said. "Mr. Kravitz died a week ago."

Startled, I gasped. My legs suddenly felt weak. *How could that be?*

My mind spinning, I let myself in the back door. I gazed around the kitchen and spotted the blue casserole dish on the counter. I picked up the dish and opened the lid. The dish was empty.

So, I guess I *did* see a ghost. But when people ask, I always say I never saw one.

I guess the truth is, I hope I never see another one.

R.L. STINE is one of the bestselling children's authors in history. Now in its thirtieth year, Goosebumps has sold more than 400 million books. The Goosebumps series made R.L. Stine a worldwide publishing celebrity (and *Jeopardy!* answer). His other popular children's book series include Fear Street (recently revived as a feature film trilogy), The Garbage Pail Kids, Mostly Ghostly, The Nightmare Room, and Rotten School. Other titles include *It's the First Day of School . . . Forever, A Midsummer Night's Scream, Young Scrooge,* and two picture books with Marc Brown—*The Little Shop of Monsters* and *Mary McScary.* R.L. lives in New York City with his wife, Jane, an editor and publisher.

VICTORY AFTER DEFEAT

by Soman Chainani

When I was a kid, my dad used to call me "America's Storyteller" because I couldn't open my mouth without it turning into an epic, dramatic tale, usually involving unicorns or dinosaurs.

"Where's your lunch box?" my mom might ask, which would prompt a story about pterodactyls that I suspected were living in our basement, both as a distraction from the fact that I'd lost the lunch box and because I was pretty sure there were Jurassic beasts taking up residence in our house.

Everyone told me I would be a writer one day. It wasn't just the only thing I was good at. It was what I was put on this earth to do from day one. Spin fantasies. Tell tall tales. Turn missing lunch boxes into pterodactyls.

But there was a time where I gave up on being a writer.

Too many things had gone wrong, too many rugs pulled out from under me.

Until that point, everything had been a little too charmed. I'd come out of film school at twenty-six years old, a hot-shot writer/ director signed to a big Hollywood agency, and was on track to direct my first feature film in London the following summer. Off the heat of that project—a romantic comedy about two Indian families warring over a marriage—I'd been hired to write an animated movie for Sony Pictures about Indian elephants and given a deal to create my own television show about a divorcing couple who runs a wedding house in northern England. I woke up every day with too much to do but in my own creative heaven where every dream seemed to come to life.

"America's Storyteller" was on his path.

Backing up a bit, it's worth noting that being a writer was my only real option for a job, because I was fired from everything else. I wasn't sure how to be a professional writer when I was young. It didn't seem like a viable option for a career, even if it was the only thing I was good at. So I tried other, more respectable jobs . . . none of which worked out. Pharmaceutical consultant? Fired. Production assistant? Fired. Website copywriter? Fired. Not because I was so terrible at any of these jobs, but because I'd inevitably hide in a corner and work on a new screenplay instead of the spreadsheet or PowerPoint I'd been asked to deliver. Writing was my higher calling, and it took me a long while to accept that I wouldn't be happy doing anything else. The universe rewarded my commitment by gilding a path to film school and beyond, a life that once stutter-stepped between failures now parading through open doors of movies and TV deals.

Then one frigid February morning, I woke up in my apartment in New York to two messages from London. First message: the movie I was supposed to direct would now be put on hold, because one of the financiers was going into bankruptcy. Second message: the animated film was canceled, since the production company had lost its deal with Sony. The TV show about the wedding house didn't last long either, sunk by personnel changes at the production company a couple weeks later.

The worst part was, given the projects were all in fairly early stages, I wouldn't be paid in any real way.

Not only did I not have a job, but I also had no income.

Looking back now, I remember having a strange reaction to all this. Not misery or depression or anxiety . . . but relief. The feeling that it was all too good to be true, so when the glass house shattered, I could retreat to a safe thought: "Of course it wasn't real. Of course it wasn't going to happen." When you don't believe you deserve the opportunities you're given, eventually the universe will take them away.

For the next year, I ambled about aimlessly, finding work as a tutor and an essay editor, helping everyone else with their writing but doing none of my own.

Somehow I convinced myself that I was a tutor for life, that facilitating the writing of people not myself was my true calling. In my darkest days, I'd go to a bar twice a week for midnight karaoke, even though I don't drink, don't sing, and don't like to stay up late. Even now, I can't understand what I was thinking, other than I was seeking an escape hatch, a portal into another life that wasn't mine.

Then came a fever. A ten-day, raging storm that sent my temperature rocketing over one hundred degrees without any other symptoms. A steady bout of chills and delirium. I didn't bother going to the doctor. I knew what the fever was—my body revolting against the life I'd accepted for it. On day eleven, I found myself alone in an AMC movie theater in the middle of the afternoon, watching a Céline Dion documentary, wondering what it would be like to be

Céline, to have a purpose, a mission, a calling in life that actually was answered. To be an artist with the courage to make art, instead of a failed artist who'd so easily accepted his fate.

A week later I was in London, back to clean up the wreckage of the lost projects and convince my British film agent to keep me on, despite the lack of work and income. (He didn't.) One afternoon, I was wandering through Regent's Park, with no agenda, no plan, no anything, just empty time and space, and I had a sudden image pop into my head of a girl in black falling through the sky into a pink castle and a girl in pink falling through the sky into a black castle. It was so sharp and arresting that it stopped me cold. Such symmetry and vibrance in a single picture. I had no idea what it meant, but as the afternoon went on, the edges of the picture filled in—two schools, one for good, one for evil, and two girls, a princess and a witch, falling into the wrong castles. By the end of the afternoon, I had names—Sophie, Agatha. By the end of the week, I had the story, the world, the mythology, as if all this time that I'd been tutoring and singing at midnight bars, my subconscious had been working out a creative volcano and was just waiting for me to give it the freedom to erupt.

In my head I knew it was a book, not a screenplay, but it was also a book I refused to write.

For one thing, I'd never written a book. I'd tried here and there, but I found the experience lonely and scary, a commitment to years of work that might result in nothing. A screenplay was easier, shallower, less . . . intense. To write a book was to commit to my imagination, to the depths inside me, to another world.

So instead of writing *The School for Good and Evil*, instead of plunging into the Endless Woods . . . I flirted with it instead. I wrote outlines and treatments and synopses, big proposals for a book, but no book.

I was afraid. I was afraid of writing. After three canceled projects, the idea of giving myself to something fully again was too hard to take. The equivalent of a broken heart that's locked itself up.

But hope is a funny thing. Even when you've surrendered it, deep inside, the spark of flame is always there, looking for its tinder. Why else would I spend hours a day brainstorming character names and class schedules and maps, if I had no intention of ever following through on it? I wrote no prose, no chapters, no story, but slowly but surely, I was dipping my toe into the waters of another world.

A year later, I sent my agent a ninety-page collection of . . . thoughts. That's the best way to describe it: a scrapbook of *The School for Good and Evil*. Looking back, it was a ridiculous gambit. There was nothing to sell. Just the musings of a writer too pen-shy to write. And yet, she saw what it was . . . She saw how much commitment I had to the world if I could just give myself the permission to write it.

Later that month, she sent the scrapbook to seventeen publishers. Sixteen of them passed on it, with the predictable response: there's no book here. The seventeenth bought the idea, hook, line, and sinker, and I was instantly signed up to write three books, without a single word of any of them having been written.

What fortune. What a dose of luck. It's punch-drunk silly, really. Like winning the lottery when someone else bought your ticket.

But looking back, I like to think that the world knew I was lost. That there would be no happiness, no future as a writer without a little help. I'd lost faith in myself, in my art, in my talent, and yet, I was still there, at the edges of the water, flicking at it, searching for a sign to wade in.

This wasn't just a sign. This was a command.

And yet, even still, I remember asking my friends and family a parade of stupid questions—do I really want to write a novel? Won't I be lonely? What about my dream of directing movies? Cold-eyed stares greeted me in response. The kinds of stares you give a tutor/failed karaoke singer who's questioning whether he should follow his real life's dream.

But deep inside, I knew the answers, and eventually, I was smart enough to stop puttering around and get to work. Once I started, I never looked back. Ten years and six books later, I have such sympathy and admiration for that lost, shambling version of myself who had universes bubbling in his mind, universes frantic to find expression—and yet had somehow convinced himself that he was meant to do anything on this earth but write.

If there's one thing I've learned about hope, it's that the universe is always conspiring to help you be the best version of yourself possible. To bring you into alignment with your higher purpose and your higher self. The question is whether you resist it or whether you have the courage to become who you're meant to be, to live out your life's story, even though it might be bigger than you can consciously imagine. At some point, you accept your fate. You accept that you're a piece of the puzzle and not the whole puzzle.

In my case, I'd gotten so out of alignment that the universe threw me a bone. But once I had permission to write *The School for Good and Evil*, I gave my blood, sweat, and tears to it, this time believing I deserved the opportunity I'd been given.

Sometimes you need to lose the thing you love to find it again.

It happens with athletes who burn out from their sports. It happens to best friends who start to take each other for granted. It happens with talents that feel more like pressure than fun. It's a fact of life. In my case, I had to fail as a writer before I could become one. I had to hunger for what I'd lost before I could walk through that door a second time. And that chance always comes back around. The same way love always comes back around, just when you thought it'd left you.

I'm not afraid to write anymore. I'm afraid to *not* write. Because once you have a taste of how big your life can be, how fresh and new . . . how can you go back to the old one?

SOMAN CHAINANI is the *New York Times* bestselling author of the School for Good and Evil series. The fairy-tale saga has sold over three million copies, has been translated into thirty languages, and is a major motion picture from Netflix, which Soman executive produced. Soman's latest book, *Beasts and Beauty*, was an instant *New York Times* bestseller and will soon be published in ten languages. It is his seventh *New York Times* bestseller in a row.

Soman is a graduate of Harvard University and received his MFA in film from Columbia University. Every year, he visits schools around the world to speak to kids and share his secret: that reading is the path to a better life. You can visit Soman at SomanChainani.com.

MY FAVORITE PHOTOGRAPH

by Veera Hiranandani

If I had to choose one photograph to represent my childhood, it would be this one: I'm standing outside at school, around eight or nine years old, surrounded by four of my closest friends at the time, and we're all in the same class. For some reason, the picture is black and white, even though I'm not *that* old. Our mouths form the shape of O's because we're singing. Our eyes squint into the sun as our arms drape around each other's shoulders. There's a male teacher sitting next to us strumming a guitar and a female teacher facing us who also sings. We wear T-shirts and jeans, and every single one of us— the boys, the girls, the women, the men—have long, loose hair. We seem completely immersed in the moment. I'm not sure if it was an organized performance or just a bit of spontaneous fun. I don't even remember the exact moment captured in the photograph, but back then I had many moments like this one.

This picture was taken at the elementary school I attended from first through fourth grade. It was a small progressive, independent school in Connecticut called the Learning Community. We all called it LC. A few of my parents' friends had started the school. Let me write that again in case you missed it—the school was started by my parents' friends. Which sort of means that one day a few of them got together and said, "Hey, let's start a really awesome school!" and my parents were like "Cool!" and then they sent my sister and me there for four years. They were some of the most foundational, inspiring, and hopeful years of my life.

I don't have too many photographs from LC, but several mental snapshots come to me when I think about this time, and I think about it often. The memories I have are not in black and white. They bloom into my consciousness like rainbow-colored bursts of watercolor paint. I never get tired of revisiting them.

Here are a few more: I'm about to go on a camping trip, one of the several camping trips I went on with my class. I've got my sleeping bag tucked under my arm and a backpack slung over my shoulder. I'm standing in the parking lot, where my parents have just dropped me off. It's early in the morning. I watch one of our teachers, or a parent, or someone who was both, go through the checklist. Bread, hot dogs, peanut butter, jelly, marshmallows, milk, cereal, and water—check! Sleeping bags, clothes, and tents—check! First aid kit—check! Guitars—check! We pile into cars (and I really do mean pile; it was the seventies) and head off to Pound Ridge Reservation.

When we get there, we set up camp in one of the lean-tos (small open shelters) and spend the day hiking through the trails. We ramble over the paths and hills and rocks. We discover fallen trees, caves, flowers, squirrels, birds, frogs, and turtles. We swim in our underwear and lie on rocks in the sun to dry off. We all somehow make it back to the camp without losing anyone. There we do all the classic camping things. We roast hot dogs on sticks and tell ghost stories, and at least one of the teachers has a guitar and plays song after song. It eventually ends in a round of "Leaving on a Jet Plane" by John Denver. We fall asleep under the roof of the lean-to in our sleeping bags. The ground is hard, but I know I'll sleep because I'm exhausted from the day. The last thing I remember is falling asleep as the stars glow through the pine trees against the dark sky, which I can see through the shelter opening.

In another one, there's more tangled hair tumbling down my back. My fingernails are dirty, and the mud stains on my jeans soak through to the skin on my knees. I kneel in the dirt in front of a gravestone, clutching thick, paperless crayons. I press a large sheet of newsprint against the front of the gravestone, rubbing the side of the crayon against it. I take a print and then do another. As I rub the crayon, I think about the name of the person on the gravestone. It's windy and cold, but I don't care because I'm so engrossed in the project. I want my rubbings to look good to honor the dead. I think about the names and the lengths of the lives I'm recording. I'm a little frightened, but fascinated and curious.

In another, we take a weeklong winter trip to a place called Nature's Classroom. We stay in bunks and learn how to tap trees for sap, make maple syrup, and track animal footprints in the snow. One morning, we walk along the circumference of a large frozen lake. We all hold on to a rope and stay in a wiggly line. I remember passing a few ducks swimming in a hole in the ice toward the middle of the lake. I wonder if they're cold. We find a beaver lodge. We watch fish swimming under our feet.

In another memory, we shape and glaze pottery, so much pottery. In another, we write a play, construct and paint sets for it, direct and perform it. In another, we create a restaurant as a fundraiser, write up menus, and cook and serve food for our parents. In others, we sit quietly on beanbag chairs in the classroom as we write in our journals. We put on science fairs. We study foods, religions, and cultures from around the world. Even in the youngest grades, we discuss politics and human rights. In another, it's so nice outside, the teachers decide that recess should last all afternoon.

I had seven other kids in my class. We went through all the grades together. It was truly an extended family. During these years, I experienced the longest state of happiness that I possibly ever will. I know it was lucky and rare to have this time. It is my base. It's the roots from where much of who I am today started to form and grow. Happiness, as one gets older, is usually tempered with the complex challenges of life. In a way, you learn to appreciate the good times more because you know they're temporary. I also know many people do not have happy childhoods, but for these four years, I had the privilege of being loved, seen, and part of something completely. There were so many days filled with creativity, wonder, possibility, and hope. Many of the friends I had in school were my parents' friends' kids, and our lives blended into a fluid space. School was home was life was school. Of course, it wasn't perfect. I had conflicts with friends and the common frustrations one might feel as a first-through-fourth grader, but honestly, I remember very little of them.

Cue the sound of screeching brakes.

It had to end. Everything does eventually, even the bad things, but enrollment at the school was dwindling in the upper grades, and my parents also worried that I might not be getting enough of a well-rounded education. They were partly right, because when I changed schools, I was technically behind in some areas of math and science. But did anyone at my new school know what it was like to spend a winter morning holding hands with your classmates as you walked the perimeter of a snow-covered lake under a canopy of tree branches, as the sun rose and fish swam under your feet? Long division could never replace that.

So in fourth grade, when my class graduated, we all went our separate ways to separate school districts. Over the years, the Learning Community evolved into a preschool, and the truth is that if I had stayed and we had all continued on as a class of eight, there might have been more conflicts and growing pains. Or, if the school grew in numbers, new students and older-kid concerns would have complicated things. Perhaps I might have started to feel limited or bored. But none of this happened because I left before it could.

Cut to me in fifth grade. These are my memory snapshots of that first year: I walk in a single-file line toward the end through a long maze of hallways. Nobody speaks. It's hard to stay in line as we round the corners, but I try because the teacher calls out anyone who talks or steps out of line. I wonder why she seems to have so little trust in us?

Once, during a test, I get up to go to the bathroom. The teacher reprimands me in the middle of class. She wants to know why in the world would I go to the bathroom during a test? And if it was that urgent, why wouldn't I raise my hand and ask first? I stand there feeling ashamed and embarrassed. I want to tell her that I never had rules like this at my old school and I'm confused and I need a little more time to get used to things. But I don't. I just sit down, cheeks burning, and finish the test.

Here's another. I sit in my classroom during lunch while my teachers discuss my performance. I have two teachers in the fifth grade. They are called "team" teachers, but they don't seem to like each other very much or enjoy being on the same team. One is nicer than the other. The nice teacher, who teaches English and social studies, has recommended that I move up a level. The other teacher, who teaches math and science, has recommended that I don't. I watch them debate and wonder why I'm here for the discussion. I also wonder why I can't just move up a level in English and social studies, but not in math and science. According to the not-so-nice teacher, you have to move up in all subjects at the same time, so it's decided that I don't move up in any.

Or I'm on a playground sitting on a bench by myself as I observe the groups gathered around me. I see a girl sitting on a rock near the edge of the playground. She's also alone. She squints at me, and I smile. She just stares back, and as I try to summon up the courage to raise my hand and wave hi, she throws a pebble at me and runs away.

I also remember that none of the kids or teachers can say my last name correctly. No one asks me how to pronounce it, and I'm too shy to correct anyone. Once, at lunch, I'm asked where my name is "from." I say it's an Indian name, and one kid says "Ahhhhh" while he pats his mouth. I realize he thinks I'm Native American, and I know that if I were Native American, I would still feel awful. Another kid asks me if I worship cows and laughs at me when I don't answer.

Needless to say, the first year at my new school didn't go so well. One of the biggest adjustments was how both my racial and religious backgrounds leaped to the forefront of my identity. I was asked multiple questions about my Indian name, my background, and how I could be Indian and Jewish and Hindu at the same time. I didn't know the answer. I had never been asked this question before. At my new school, even though it was much larger, there were maybe two kids who were Jewish, and no one in my class who had an Indian background, let alone both. It seemed that I was the only person like me for miles and miles. It made me look at myself, my Indian American dad and my Jewish American mom, in a new way. It was the first time I realized that these aspects of my identity were going to be treated differently depending on the community I was in.

Being "different" isn't a bad thing. We're all different in one way or another. Humanity is incredibly diverse, but that recognition of the world's diversity doesn't exist in every community. What's interesting is that I was the only child with my particular background in my old school *and* my new school, but I was treated differently in each community. Over time, I've come to understand that the responsibility of inclusivity lies with the majority because they have more power. There are many communities where white, Christian, heterosexual, neurotypical, or nondisabled people make up the majority, like the communities at both of my schools. But how do they treat what they perceive as differences? Do they respect differences, celebrate them, incorporate them into the fabric of one community where everyone is different and also similar? Or do they reject and exclude out of the fear of losing a certain kind of power?

These questions stayed with me as I continued in school and as an adult. As I moved up in my new school, I found my way. I got involved in gymnastics, theater, and art. I wrote pieces for the literary magazine. I lost myself in books when I needed a break from the real world. I wish I could tell you that at my new school I eventually found a space where I recaptured those Learning Community days, but I didn't—not that year, nor in middle school, nor high school. Over time I adjusted and made some good friends, but I never felt completely accepted or comfortable. I continued my love of creating art, however. Writing stories, painting, and putting on plays was where I could tap into the freedom I had experienced at LC, and I remained involved in all those things year after year. It's probably why I'm a writer today.

When I look back, I've wondered if spending those years at LC in such a free and positive space sort of ruined me for the "regular" world, or somehow raised my expectations too high so that a lot of my schooling after that could only be a disappointment, but I don't think so. It taught me that being creative, open-hearted, and connected to nature was how I could carry what I learned at LC wherever I went, that it was mine and no one could take it away. It was the way I empowered myself during that first lonely year in fifth grade and how I still do.

I decided to go to college in a big city because I felt that I'd be more likely to find diverse and open-minded spaces. In some ways, I found what I was looking for, and in some ways, I didn't. These questions and feelings, however, remained with me and became the genesis of my first book, *The Whole Story of Half a Girl*.

Often we are told that when we go through more difficult times, that's when we become stronger, understand the world more clearly, and prevail. But that's not what I'm going to tell you here. Yes, some adversity can build strength. It can toughen you up and prepare you for challenges that we all face. Too much adversity can also beat you down. The kind of struggles I went through weren't that unusual. Many people go through struggles like mine, and many people go through a lot worse. We do need to get a little beaten up by the world to understand it more clearly and to develop a resilience that helps us survive tougher times. But often, the reason we dust ourselves off and keep going is because we feel hopeful that there's something better ahead. The reason we do this is because we've had a moment (or hopefully more than a moment) in our lives when we've connected with the center of who we are, when we've felt fully accepted, when we've felt like we're not only enough, but more than enough.

So think back on your life. When have you been the happiest? The most free? More *you* than you've ever been? That's what gives you the ultimate strength to push past something difficult. It's the strength you build in those moments that helps get you through. That strength is gold.

Because of LC, I know what I need to feel happy and accepted, and I know I'm worthy of that. When I'm going through something hard or doubting myself and feeling powerless or not enough, I go to that place, that photograph of my tangled hair blowing all around as I sing loudly (and by the way, I'm not a very good singer), surrounded by friends and guitars, not worrying what anyone thinks. I'm just being me to the core, and that's just fine. That's what gives me the most strength and hope for my own future.

Most of us can remember a moment like that photograph, a freeze-frame of beauty before a new worry, doubt, or fear has come our way. Maybe this moment for you was before a difficult time or after, but if you can think of a period when you experienced a clearing of space, like a field of wildflowers discovered unexpectedly after climbing up a mountain, a place where perhaps you felt your essence in all its glory, don't forget to capture it in some way—draw it, write about it, take a mental snapshot. This moment might only be a few minutes, or an hour, or a day, or four years, but it doesn't matter how long it was, only that you can remember it when you need it, like a photograph in your pocket. It will give you the clarity and strength to move forward in a direction that honors you—the real you—full of hope and possibility.

VEERA HIRANANDANI is the author of *How to Find What You're Not Looking For* (Kokila) and *The Night Diary* (Kokila), which has received many awards including the 2019 Newbery Honor, the 2019 Walter Dean Myers Honor Award, and the 2018 Malka Penn Award for Human Rights in Children's Literature. She is also the author of *The Whole Story of Half a Girl* (Yearling), which was named a Sydney Taylor Notable Book and a South Asia Book Award Highly Commended Book, and the chapter book series Phoebe G. Green (Penguin Workshop). She earned her MFA in fiction writing at Sarah Lawrence College. A former book editor at Simon & Schuster, she now teaches creative writing at Sarah Lawrence College's Writing Institute and is working on her next novel.

THE BOY IN THE BACK OF THE CLASS

by Ronald L. Smith

When I was a kid in middle school, I used to sit in the back of the classroom and read fantasy books.

No one ever seemed to notice that I was doing this. I think I must have placed the book in my notebook and pretended like I was studying. I wasn't. I was reading about Bilbo Baggins and his adventures in *The Hobbit,* traveling to the moon in *The Wonderful Flight to the Mushroom Planet,* and stepping into a magical wardrobe and finding myself in The Chronicles of Narnia. I was swept away by these books, and it's what led me to become a writer. But in those days, that seemed like an impossible goal.

I used to think that writers were some sort of supernatural beings, like a cross between the wizard Merlin and Spider-Man, my favorite superhero when I was a kid. Writers created worlds and filled them with magical creatures. They made nations rise and fall. They left heroes dangling on the edge of a cliff. And they kept me up all night, reading under the covers with a flashlight because my parents had warned me several times to turn out the light. This was back before the internet and social media. There was no way you could actually meet a real writer. They were in an ivory tower somewhere, working on their next masterpiece.

Or at least that's what twelve-year-old me thought. Little did I know that years later, I would go on to write my own books for kids. In fact, I still can't believe it!

I don't really remember why I didn't pay attention in school. Maybe I was bored. Maybe I thought I knew more than the teachers. *Wrong*. But, when I think back on it, there *was* a reason. One that makes a lot more sense than just being bored.

I couldn't see the blackboard.

This was before whiteboards and computer-assisted screens. Do teachers even use chalk and blackboards anymore? Have you ever erased a blackboard? Kids used to clap the erasers together and create a big cloud of white chalk that ended up everywhere. (Not that I ever did that. Okay. Maybe once.).

Anyway, I don't know why I never told my teachers I couldn't read the words on the blackboard. I must have been too shy. At some point—maybe my grades were slipping—my teachers must have talked to my parents about my not participating in class. Or maybe I finally confessed to my mom and dad that I couldn't see the blackboard. (I don't remember telling them that, but I imagine it could have happened.) So, you know what my parents did?

They took me to the eye doctor.

The Eye Doctor!

I was scared.

What would the doctor say?

Was there really something wrong with me?

Would I need an operation?

Fortunately, all of my fears were just the result of a creative kid's overactive imagination.

So, do you want to know what my problem *really* was?

Sure you do.

I needed glasses.

Now, you might think that this was a relief, considering all of my other unfounded fears. But it really wasn't. You may as well have told me I was about to go into surgery. This was in the 1970s. (I know. The Dark Ages.) Only goofy kids wore glasses, I thought. *Not true.*

I could hear the teasing already: *Hey, four-eyes! Yo, Professor!*

I even thought a bully might snatch my glasses from my face and step on them!

Well, none of that happened.

But I knew that glasses would just make me retreat even further into my shell, like some kind of turtle.

I remember going to the doctor to pick up my glasses when they arrived. On the car ride there, I didn't know what to expect. All I knew was that these new glasses were going to be big and black and clunky, like some kind of weird contraption on my face. I'd probably look like a monster from one of the sci-fi stories I liked to read.

But you know what?

I was wrong.

They actually fit my face quite well. I remember when I looked in the mirror at the optometrist's office. It was still me, just a little . . . different. And on the car ride home, I noticed something.

I could see farther than the front of my nose!

The whole world came into focus. When we got home, I jumped on my bike and rode all around the neighborhood. It was an adventure. Everything was new and shiny.

Wow, I never knew the water in the community pool was so blue.

Hey, that TV show Lost in Space *really looks better now.*

Even the words in this book I'm reading are clearer.

It was like the scene in that old movie *The Wizard of Oz*. Have you ever seen it? The movie starts out in black and white but bursts into color once Dorothy, the main character, steps into this land called Oz.

That's what it was like for me. Except for the flying monkeys. Look it up.

So, even though my eyesight was now as sharp as an eagle's, I still had one problem.

I had to be *seen* in my new glasses.

Like I said already, I was a shy kid and had trouble meeting new people and making friends. Maybe it was because we moved around so much when I was little. Every time I made a new friend, we had to move away. My dad was in the air force, and we lived in about six or seven states before I became a teenager.

I don't remember what that first day in school was like with my new glasses. I knew that I could see the blackboard . . . finally. But I was still a little hesitant to be seen.

I think one of the main reasons was because there were girls I liked, and I didn't want them to see me with glasses. I was never interested in wearing contact lenses. It always seemed scary to me. Who wants to put a finger in their eye to take out a lens? That seemed nuts.

I wasn't into sports back then, but that didn't prevent me from having to go to gym class. I hated it. But you know what happened? I actually became better at a few things because my vision was sharper. I even made a few baskets when we played basketball because I could actually *see the net*. Same with baseball. Before, when the ball came speeding my way, all I wanted to do was jump out of the way. But with glasses, I focused on that incoming rocket of a ball with laser-like precision. And I actually got on base a few times. But don't get me started on climbing a rope. I still don't know if I could do it, glasses or not!

When I look back on it now, this all seems silly. But it wasn't back then. It was deadly serious. That's what adults forget sometimes. All of those moments you're going through that *they* think might be nothing *are* a big deal to you. These experiences are going to make you a stronger person in the future. They shape who you are and who you will become.

But I didn't know that back then.

All I knew was that I liked Danette Saunders, and when she finally saw me with my glasses, she said, "Hey, those look cool."

I couldn't believe it.

All this time I was so embarrassed to be seen, but people didn't really seem to care about it. This is something that has stuck with me. When you're really stressing over something, sometimes it turns out to be not that big of a deal. You just have to get on with it. But other times, you do have to ask for help, and that's okay, too.

That boost of confidence from Danette made me feel good about myself and less nervous. I wonder if she remembers me. Danette, if you're out there, thanks!

Over time, I became more confident and started raising my hand in class. I even started writing my own stories and kept a notebook with me at all times, where I would scribble down ideas. All those notebooks are long gone now. Moving every two years was not a good way to keep track of things. I've always wondered what it would be like if I could read those stories now. When I visit schools, I always tell young people to print out their stories and keep them in a special place so they won't lose them. Having them on the computer isn't enough. Computers do break down now and then, after all.

Anyway, wearing glasses became a big part of me, as vital as an arm or a leg. I became more active in class, especially English—where I never had to study the vocabulary words because I read so much on my own—and I really began to enjoy it a lot more. We used to read aloud sometimes, and for some reason, when it was my turn, I started giving different voices to the characters, like I did when reading to myself. I got really good at it. So much so that I remember my teacher saying: "So, if you're all good today, we can have Ron read a chapter."

I don't recall what we were reading. Maybe it was *The Last of the Mohicans*? *The Deerslayer*? "The Legend of Sleepy Hollow"? It's all a blur. *Blur*. Well, it wasn't a blur back then, because I was wearing glasses. See what I did there?

Today, I can't even imagine a life without my glasses. When I was a kid, I expected everything to change when I learned I had to wear them. And things did change . . . for the better. Not only could I navigate the world a bit easier, I was also able to look into the mirror and accept myself, glasses and all.

So, if you're out there and feeling embarrassed or shy about a change you have to make to your appearance—whether it's glasses, braces, a hearing aid, or anything else—just remember: it's who you are on the inside that really matters.

Now go check out *The Wizard of Oz*.

• • •

RONALD L. SMITH is an award-winning writer of children's literature, including the novels *Black Panther: The Young Prince* and *Hoodoo*, which earned him the 2016 Coretta Scott King–John Steptoe Award for New Talent. His latest projects are two new Black Panther novels for Marvel and *Where the Black Flowers Bloom*, a fantasy based on African folklore and myths.

THE FRIEND WHO CHANGED MY LIFE

by Pam Muñoz Ryan

In fifth grade, my family moved across town. I was filled with the hope of my own room, a nice teacher, and with any luck, friends. I received my own room and the nice teacher. The friends part wasn't that easy.

I hated being the new kid at school.

I was tall for my age and already wore a size nine shoe—an awkward atrocity. My brown hair was kept wholesomely off my face with hair clips. How was I to know that ponytails and short bangs were the rage at this school? Since I hadn't yet adopted the no-socks look, my sense of style didn't blend, either. I wanted to fit in, but I wore my vulnerability like a new pair of white shoes, all too ready to be scuffed up. A bully took advantage.

Her name was Theresa. She was tiny, wiry, and loud, with blond bangs and tightly pulled-back hair. I swore she walked with a deliberate swagger just to get her ponytail to swing from side to side. For a reason unknown to me, she decided that I was worthy of her attention, and every day she waltzed up to me and kicked me in the shins or the back of the legs. At first, I wondered if this was some sort of new-kid initiation, but she didn't let up. I could expect a wallop when

I least expected it—while I was standing in line after recess, on my way out of the girls' bathroom, or as I pushed my lunch tray along the counter in front of the cafeteria ladies. *Bam!* Theresa was smart and quick. No teacher ever saw her, and within a week, my legs were bruised black, blue, purple, and green.

My mom noticed the marks, but I told her that I played on the jungle gym at recess every day and had hit them on the bars. I could tell she was suspicious of my story, so I promised I'd play somewhere else. I knew that if I kept coming home with mottled legs, though, one of my parents would eventually go to my teacher. I could only imagine the price I'd have to pay at school if I were the new kid *and* a crybaby tattletale.

I used to lie in bed every night dreading going to school and hoping that things would get better. I tried to figure out complicated routes to walk from one place to another so Theresa couldn't get to me easily. I had a roundabout method of getting to my classroom in the morning, which involved walking outside the fenced schoolyard and entering the grounds at the opposite end of the campus, then working my way through the kindergarten playground. At recess and lunch, I stayed in the open spaces on the grassy field so that if I saw Theresa coming, I could at least run. That worked, some of the time. One day on the playground, as she was about to close in on me again, I bolted away, fast. I glanced over one shoulder and, with relief, didn't see her and thought she had given up. I stopped abruptly and turned around, unaware that Theresa had been running full-speed toward me. She didn't expect my sudden stop and slammed into me and fell to the ground. A group of kids standing nearby laughed. Angry, she leaped up and began kicking me with a fury. A scrape on my knee reopened, and blood trickled down my leg. As much as I wanted to, I didn't cry.

Mary Lou, also in the fifth grade, was the tallest and biggest girl in the entire school. She was sturdy and big-boned and strong, with red hair and thousands of freckles. No one ever messed with her. When Mary Lou shoved through the crowd of kids and took my elbow, everyone backed away, including Theresa.

Mary Lou ushered me to the girls' bathroom. As I stood there, shaking, she took a wad of paper towels, wet them, handed them to me, and pointed to my bloodied leg.

"So, Theresa's been bothering you."

I nodded, hoping that the next words out of Mary Lou's mouth would be, "Well, I'm going to take care of her for you." I had visions of having a personal hero to protect me—fantasies of Mary Lou escorting me around the school with a protective arm over my shoulder and clobbering anyone who came near me.

Instead, Mary Lou said, "You can't let her keep doing this to you. She's never going to stop unless you make her stop. Get it?"

I didn't really get it. I shook my head.

"Listen, she's a pain. But if you don't stick up for yourself, things will get worse. You know that, don't you?"

How could it get worse? And what did Mary Lou mean about sticking up for myself? Did she want me to *fight* Theresa? That idea terrified me more than being kicked every day.

"I'm not kidding," said Mary Lou. "And if you don't *do* something, I'm not going to help you again. Understand?" She made a fist and held it in front of my face.

I gulped. Things could *definitely* get worse. "Yes," I whispered.

"Okay then, get back out there."

Now? Did she mean stand up for myself *right now*?

I walked back to the playground with Mary Lou smugly following behind. I couldn't see a way out of the situation. In front of me was Theresa, and in back of me was Mary Lou. The first bell rang, and kids began to assemble on the blacktop in front of the classrooms in their assigned lines. In a few minutes, the second bell would ring and teachers would walk out and get their students for class. The yard-duty teacher was still out on the grassy field, blowing her whistle and rounding up the stragglers.

Theresa stood in a huddle of girls. Mary Lou nudged me toward her. I had never instigated a fight before in my life. I had never hit anyone and didn't have an inkling of what to do. My insides shook worse than my outsides. When Theresa saw me approaching, she set her mouth in a grim line, marched toward me, and swung her leg back to haul off and kick me. I jumped back to avoid the kick. I made a fist and flailed my arm wildly, in some sort of ridiculous motion. In a miraculous blow, I caught Theresa in the nose, and blood sprayed across her clothes. I don't know which of us was more surprised.

I don't remember what happened next. I know we brawled on the blacktop. Gritty sand scraped the skin on my arms, and I would notice the burns later. As we rolled over and over, tiny pebbles got embedded in my face. One of them made a substantial puncture that didn't heal for weeks. In a matter of minutes, someone had retrieved the yard-duty teacher, and she corralled and ceremoniously walked us to the principal's office. Devastated, I hung my head.

Sitting on the bench outside the principal's office and waiting to be called in, I worried about several things. Would the school tell my parents? What would our punishment be? What would Theresa do to get back at me? What would the other kids think? Branded, I was now a bad girl.

The yard-duty teacher deposited us in two chairs, side by side, in the principal's office and placed the referral slip on his desk. Our principal was a balding man with glasses and a kind, grandfatherly face. He seemed happy to see us.

"Well, girls, I want you to put your heads together and decide what your punishment should be while I make a phone call."

He picked up the phone, and as he made his call, I stared at his desk. I realized I could read the referral slip upside down. The yard-duty teacher had written, "Benched for one week."

Theresa leaned toward me and whispered, remorsefully, "I guess we should be benched for two weeks." She felt worse than I suspected.

I glared at her and shook my head no.

The principal put down the phone. "Well, young ladies?"

"We should be benched for a week," I blurted.

"I agree, and I don't want to see you back here anytime soon." He signed the referral and sent us back to class.

"How did you know to say one week?" she asked.

"I could read what the yard-duty teacher put on the slip. Upside down," I said.

"Wow, you can read upside down?" said Theresa, her ponytail swinging like a pendulum.

I didn't answer her.

That night I told my mother that I fell jumping rope.

Theresa and I were confined to the same green bench next to the stucco wall of the cafeteria for every recess and lunchtime. It was indisputably the Bad Kids' Bench. Kindergartners and first graders had to file by to get to their classrooms, and they always gave us a wide berth, the orderly line snaking away from us, then back in formation, as if our badness might be contagious. The bench faced the playground so the entire recess population could see who was *not privileged* enough to play. The yard-duty teacher could keep an eye on us, too, in case we decided to jump up and sneak in a game of hopscotch. Indignant, I refused to talk to Theresa, who didn't seem to have any inhibitions about being chatty.

She bragged to me about all sorts of things, but I ignored her until she said, "My mom takes me to the *big* downtown library every Tuesday after school."

I rode my bike to the small branch library near my house every weekend, but my parents both worked full-time and couldn't always manage after-school activities or driving to the main branch. The *big* library had a hundred times the selection and a huge children's room with comfy pillows. They sometimes had puppet shows, story times, free bookmarks, and writing contests.

"Yep, every single Tuesday I go to the *big* downtown library to check out as many books as I like."

Before I could feign indifference, and with sincere awe, I said, "You're lucky."

I was suddenly jealous of Theresa, but I didn't want her to know how much. I reverted to giving her the silent treatment.

The week was over soon enough. The principal never called my parents. The other kids didn't seem to care that I had been disciplined on the Bad Kids' Bench. In fact, I actually detected a reverence from some of my classmates. From then on, Theresa left me alone, and Mary Lou was my acknowledged ally. I hoped I could repay her someday.

• • •

A few weeks passed, and one of the girls in our class had a slumber party. All the fifth-grade girls were invited. We descended on the birthday girl's house with our sleeping bags, pillows, and overnight cases. Mary Lou and I set up our sleeping bags right next to each other. The night progressed happily, until someone suggested we tell ghost stories.

I hated ghost stories. I had far too active of an imagination that took me much further than the storytelling. I couldn't seem to turn off the dark, scary world. If I saw even a slightly scary movie on television, my stomach would churn for days, and I'd have to sleep with my bedside lamp on all night. Mary Lou must have felt the same, because she moved closer to me. We huddled together behind the avid listeners with our pillows almost covering our faces. There was no way *not* to listen. One girl told a particularly gruesome tale about a tree whose giant branches turned into fingers and could grab and capture children. Most of the girls squealed and clutched each other in mock terror and then ended up giggling. Already anxious, I couldn't imagine how I would get through the night. I suddenly wanted to be in my own house, in my own bed, with my parents down the hall and my trusty bedside lamp. There didn't seem to be any way out of the situation that wasn't humiliating. At least Mary Lou was by my side.

Suddenly, Mary Lou started crying. "I'm scared. I want to go home."

Mary Lou had read my mind, but she had the courage to say it.

One of the girls said, "Don't be such a baby!"

Others chimed in, "Mary Lou's a scaredy-cat!"

"I'm calling my parents," said Mary Lou through her giant sniffles.

"The baby's calling her mommy and daddy," the girls chanted.

I shivered in my sleeping bag, my stomach sick with fear. Sick that Mary Lou was leaving. Sick that I was next to a window, with a tree looming on the other side.

Mary Lou headed toward the phone and didn't seem to care about the taunting. She called her parents with her chin up, set down the phone, and methodically began packing up her things.

My sleeping area looked bare without Mary Lou's sleeping bag and blanket. A tree branch brushed against the window from the wind. I was convinced it was the same tree from the story and that I would be its next victim.

I stood up and began rolling my sleeping bag. "I'm going home, too. Mary Lou, can your dad give me a ride?"

I heard more giggles.

Then, from across the room, a small voice said, "Me too?"

Mary Lou nodded.

I secretly celebrated, knowing that we'd suffer the consequences of the gossip and finger-pointing at school on Monday, but now I didn't care. There was safety in numbers. As I dragged my things into the hallway, I saw the third person.

It was Theresa.

The three of us huddled on the front porch waiting for Mary Lou's dad. In a final cruel gesture, one of the girls turned off the porch light so we had to wait on the front steps in the dark, directly under the tree with the sprawling branches. On the other side of the door, the girls howled with laughter. I was never so grateful to see station wagon headlights.

Mary Lou's dad headed toward Theresa's house first. On the way, we were mostly quiet, but I felt happy. Happy I was going home to my own room. Happy that Mary Lou's tearful exit scene had been watered down by our group departure. I was puzzled, though, that Theresa had been frightened, too. She always seemed so tough.

In front of Theresa's house, she climbed out of the car and said, "So do you guys want to go to the library with me after school on Tuesdays? My mom drives me and she could drive you, too."

I would love to go to the big downtown library on Tuesdays after school, I thought. *But with Theresa?* My mind battled. After all, she was the enemy, wasn't she?

Theresa eagerly continued. "My mom can call your moms to make sure it's okay and everything."

I hesitated. "Are *you* going?" I asked Mary Lou.

"I can't," she said. "But you should go if you want to."

"Yeah, you can come. It's fun." Theresa sounded sincere enough.

Mary Lou elbowed me as if to say, *Go!*

I finally nodded.

It was a strange camaraderie, given our history. Theresa and I shared many trips to the library together on Tuesdays. I've often wondered if, in some odd way, Theresa's abuse had been an attempt to get my attention. She liked the library, and I always had my nose in a book, so she targeted me. Too bad for my legs that she didn't have better social skills!

Mary Lou was, and still is, my hero. If a person believes in the domino effect, the premise that one action triggers another, then I am deeply indebted to her. If she had never made me stand up to Theresa, I would have existed on the outskirts of fifth-grade society, always defenseless. I would have never gained Mary Lou's respect or had the courage to leave with her and Theresa that night at the slumber party. Instead, I would have suffered through my worst imaginings. And if it hadn't been for Mary Lou, I might not have had the opportunity or courage to accept Theresa's invitation to the downtown library on Tuesdays, which fueled my affection for books in a dramatic way.

It's sometimes easier to hold on to the possibility that things will get better if you have someone whom you can stand beside, or who you know is always standing behind you. Being Mary Lou's friend was always comforting, even when she revealed her own vulnerability. Big, strong people have fears (as do tiny, wiry people), and it often takes more courage to reveal a weakness than to cover it up. Mary Lou was confident, determined, fair-minded, and unafraid of her emotions. She fit in because she didn't try to be anything but herself.

I hoped that someday I could be just like her.

PAM MUÑOZ RYAN is the author of *Echo*, a Newbery Honor Book and winner of the Kirkus Prize. She has written over forty books, including the celebrated novels *Esperanza Rising*, *Becoming Naomi León*, *Riding Freedom*, *Paint the Wind*, *The Dreamer*, and *Mañanaland*.

THERE'S MORE TO PLAYIN' BALL THAN JUST PLAYIN' BALL

by Matt de la Peña

Mr. Prestwood was at the gate, waving for me.

It felt like I was swimming through some kind of airproof bubble as I started toward him. I'd just taken the first flight of my life, and my ears were no longer working. All the voices around me had muffled into a low hum, like when you hold a seashell up to your ear to listen to the ocean. I had a small duffel bag slung over my shoulder, packed with a toothbrush, a couple T-shirts, a tattered pair of high-tops—a crisp twenty-dollar bill, a last-minute gift from my abuela, was tucked inside my notebook. But no remedy for plugged-up ears.

"Ah, there he is," Mr. Prestwood said, taking my duffel.

I squinted, trying to make meaning out of the muted sounds coming from his mouth. "Excuse me, sir?"

He patted me on the back. "I said here you are. You made it."

I didn't want him to repeat himself again, so I nodded.

Truth be told, I'd nodded my way through much of my childhood. Whenever I found myself in an uncomfortable situation, or if someone asked me a question I didn't understand, or didn't *want* to understand, I'd simply nod my head. Like it was all good, we're on the same page, let's just move on and forget this whole thing ever happened.

I'd learned it from the best, my old man.

"You ready?" Mr. Prestwood asked, starting toward the exit.

This time I did a little lip-reading to supplement his muffled sounds. "Ready, sir."

He stopped abruptly and turned to me. "Listen, Matt. There's no need to call me *sir*. We invited you up here for the weekend. You're our guest. Understand?"

It sounded like his words were coming from some other terminal, in some other city.

I nodded, and then we were on the escalator, going up, up, up.

I knew the Prestwoods because my mom used to babysit their daughters.

My mom babysat a whole mess of kids back then. Each morning I was awakened by the doorbell as parents ushered their toddlers into our small house, or handed over crying babies, before backpedaling toward their cars, waving and blowing kisses, then driving off to their important jobs. Me and my sisters ate breakfast cereal at the table surrounded by a handful of random kids, staring at us. Another handful crawling around near our feet. After school I had to tiptoe into my own room to keep from waking up whichever kid was napping there. Sometimes one of these kids would pee my bed, too, but don't worry, don't worry, my mom had recently covered every mattress in the house with stiff plastic sheets.

Mr. Prestwood was a well-known high school basketball coach. On Fridays he was the one who did the pickup. And once he found out I was obsessed with the game, just like *he* was obsessed with the game, he started dropping little nuggets of hoop wisdom as he corralled his kids.

"Always challenge yourself, Matt. If you're not getting beat, you're not getting better."

"Quiet your mind when you take the court. The best players don't reason their way through the game, they *feel* their way through."

"Ever taken a psych class, Matt? You need to study how people think. You need to understand human motivation. There's more to playing the game of basketball than just playing basketball."

After he accepted the head coaching position at a powerhouse high school in Northern California, he'd occasionally write me letters. They were short. Some bit of hoop advice or an update about his new team. A line about my mom and how much they missed having reliable childcare. But near the end of summer, he sent a different kind of letter. It was an invitation—from both him and his wife. They wanted to know if I'd like to visit their family one weekend. They'd pay for my flight and feed me and set me up in their spare room. Mr. Prestwood would let me have a key to his high school gym. "Maybe you can even work out with my guys," he scribbled beneath his signature.

When I showed the letter to my dad, he scoffed. "Why would you wanna do that? You got food and a bedroom *here.*"

But my mom was more open to this kind of thing. To her it was an opportunity. Same thing for my abuela. And I'm pretty sure my sisters just wanted me out of the house for a couple days. Eventually the five of us wore my old man down, and one night, as I was washing dishes, he walked past me on his way to the fridge and muttered, "You do what you gotta do, all right?"

I spun around. "So it's okay? I can go?"

He shrugged and took his beer into the living room and sat back in front of the TV.

A week later, my mom was dropping me off at the airport.

Growing up, we never went anywhere. We stayed tucked inside our working-class community and put our heads down and didn't ask the world for anything special. I guess that's why I felt so strange shuffling down the jet bridge with my duffel bag, clutching my boarding pass. Even as a kid, I felt guilty for dreaming beyond my humble little life. I felt disloyal. I felt like I was turning my back on who I was supposed to be.

When we pulled into Mr. Prestwood's long driveway, we found Mrs. Prestwood sitting on the front porch with their daughters. She gave me a hug and welcomed me to their home, and then the girls led me on a grand tour, pointing out every closet, every potted plant and toy bin and family photo. I was fairly certain the younger one, Sonya, had peed my bed on at least one occasion, but I was so humbled by the Prestwoods' generosity, I was ready to forgive.

Halfway through dinner, after I'd nodded and shrugged my way through the conversation, Mrs. Prestwood covered my hand with her own hand and said in a loud, slow voice, "You can't hear a word we're saying, can you, Matt?"

I shook my head. "Not really, ma'am."

Mrs. Prestwood turned to her husband and practically shouted, "His ears are plugged up. From the flight."

"Doesn't he know how to pop them?" Sonya asked.

"He could just chew gum," her sister added.

"These girls are old pros," Mr. Prestwood said with a wink.

"I've been on thirteen flights," Sonya announced, "including one to Frankfurt, Germany, that lasted *twelve and a half hours.*"

And now Mr. and Mrs. Prestwood and their daughters were laughing, laughing, laughing. I grinned and forked in a last bite of lasagna. As I chewed, I glanced around their giant house, at the framed art hanging on every wall and the fancy chandelier and polished hardwood floors, and I was so swept up by it all, I began laughing, too, imagining that I had always lived here, with this blond, blue-eyed family, and each night after dinner we had apple pie, which Mrs. Prestwood was now dishing out with perfect little scoops of vanilla ice cream, as classical music played quietly on the speakers mounted above our heads, making it all seem like a scene from a movie.

When Mrs. Prestwood came back from putting away the ice cream, she set a small white pill in front of me and said in her loud, slow voice, "This is an antihistamine, Matt. It will help drain the fluid." I washed it down with water, and she demonstrated how I could pop my ears by pinching my nose with my thumb and forefinger and closing my mouth and blowing hard. I followed her instructions and made a big show of sucking in a deep breath, but I only pretended to blow. The whole thing seemed like a bad idea to me. What if my eardrums exploded? What if the Prestwoods had to rush me to the hospital for emergency surgery and I wasn't able to play ball with Mr. Prestwood's team?

"So . . . ?" one of the girls said, once I'd let go of my nose. "Did it work?"

I looked at all of their expectant faces.

I nodded.

They cheered, and Sonya gave me a high five, and Mrs.

Prestwood said, "You don't have to suffer in silence, Matt. You can ask us for help."

"It's going to be tough out there," Mr. Prestwood warned the following morning, on our way to the high school. "These guys are older than you. And they're coming off a league championship."

I was only half listening, though. I was more focused on the fact that my hearing had improved. It wasn't perfect, but the small white pill had made conversation possible.

"If things get too intense," he went on, "you can always take a break, understand?"

"Yes, sir."

"No harm in watching from the bleachers."

We pulled into the mostly empty parking lot, and I spotted a group of high schoolers standing around the closed green doors, waiting to be let in. There were some pretty big dudes there—all white—wearing blue-and-silver sweatshirts or hoops shorts. Some passing a basketball back and forth. Others stretching or dribbling around on the sidewalk or lobbing a ball off the concrete wall and catching it.

Mr. Prestwood fumbled with his keys as we approached the gym, saying loud enough for his team to hear, "These guys may look big and tough, but they're teddy bears."

Some of the guys chuckled, and Mr. Prestwood motioned toward the biggest guy and said, "Except Bates here. His elbows are lethal, and he has very little body control."

"Come on, Coach," Bates said in a deep, country-sounding voice. "I'm taking ballet this summer, remember?"

"Ah, the ballet class," Mr. Prestwood said. "How could I forget."

After a little more good-natured trash talk, Mr. Prestwood introduced me, telling his team that I was a family friend visiting from San Diego, and I was only going into the ninth grade.

The guys all told me their names and gave me fist bumps and little slaps on the back, and then Mr. Prestwood headed off toward the parking lot and the rest of us filed into the dark gym.

Someone flipped on the lights.

There were three full courts. All the nets were intact. All the walls were covered with championship banners. As the guys took the court—some shooting flat-footed warm-up shots, others tying their shoes or stretching—butterflies took flight inside my stomach. This had always been my favorite feeling in the world. Excitement mixed with fear, like when your roller-coaster cart *clink-clink-clink*s up to the top of the highest peak and you know it's about to go down.

A guy named Henderson split up the teams and barked out who was guarding who, and before I knew it we were sprinting up and down the court and I was sucking wind.

First time I touched the ball, I fumbled it out of bounds.

A minute later, I shot a short jumper from the left elbow that barely grazed iron.

Neither team had even scored a point yet, but I could already read it on their faces. These guys thought I was a scrub. They thought I was some weak-link hoop impostor they'd have to carry all morning as a favor to Mr. Prestwood.

But soon I got my wind back.

And my nerves quieted.

After I buried a second deep three in a row, a guy on the sideline said, "Okay, Matt, I see you."

A few plays later I picked off a lazy crosscourt pass, drove down the lane, and lofted a high-arcing floater over Bates's outstretched hand that nestled in the net, putting us up three.

It was that floater that changed things.

That's when these bigger, stronger, league-champion upper-classmen saw me for who I really was. When they stepped aside and allowed me into the guts of their game.

Truth be told, when it came to the sport of basketball, *this* was what I lived for. Not the wins or losses. Not the makes or misses. Not the lifelong friendships or any of that other rah-rah coach speak. Nah, I was consumed with the way in an instant I could so radically change the way others perceived me.

One minute I was a mop-headed, half-Mexican, underprivileged kid in hand-me-down sneakers. The next minute I was the guy they looked for on game point.

These high school kids were good. But they were good in that well-coached kind of way. They'd done all the drills. Attended all the basketball camps and paid attention during all the film sessions. But I'd learned the game on the streets. On old, flea-bitten outdoor courts and in dilapidated gyms. Which meant my game was looser. More free. I knew how and when to paint outside the lines.

If this had been a playoff game with refs, with two coaches barking out instructions from the sideline and a crowd of people in the stands, these high school guys would have had the upper hand.

But there were no coaches today.

No crowds.

This was pickup ball.

And pickup was *my* domain.

• • •

The games had just died down by the time Mr. Prestwood came back.

He held open one of the green doors, grinning as his guys all slapped hands with me on our way out of the gym, saying things like, "Yo, that crossover's nasty, though," and "You saw how he put it on Sully, right?" and "Next time Matt's with me, Coach."

It was mostly quiet as we drove back.

When Mr. Prestwood pulled into his driveway and shut off the car, he didn't get out right away. He stared through the windshield, at his garage door, nodding to himself, like he was following some kind of secret conversation.

"I remember when your mom first told me you played," he finally said. "I had one of my assistants watch you in summer league. He said you could really shoot it." He turned to face me. "But what I saw out there today, Matt . . . You have a chance to do something really special with this game. And I keep thinking, God, if only this kid had some real coaching."

I shifted in my seat. "You were watching us?"

He smiled, pulling his keys from the ignition. "We have a coaching booth near the top of the bleachers. I always grab a coffee from across the street, then climb up to the booth to watch. The guys all know. Why do you think there's never any arguing?"

Something about this conversation made me feel like I was going to cry.

I think it was his use of the word *special*. I'd spent all my life trying to get close to a word like that.

Or it could have been something more cynical. Like deep down, I knew he was wrong about me. And I couldn't bear the thought of his disappointment when he realized it.

• • •

That night, during dinner, Mrs. Prestwood clinked her fork against her water glass and said, "Girls, there's something we'd like to discuss."

Mr. Prestwood set down his milk glass and looked at me, before turning to his two daughters. "Your mom and I have been batting around an idea. We think Matt would really benefit from some additional structure. And I'm not just talking about athletic structure."

"We're only in the exploratory phase right now," Mrs. Prestwood said. "But we want to be transparent with you two right from the beginning. How would you feel if we invited Matt to come and live with us?"

The girls looked at me, vigorously nodding their heads.

"This would only be during the school year, of course," Mr. Prestwood added. "If Matt and his parents are even interested."

I sat there frozen in shock.

"He could live in my room!" Sonya blurted out.

Her sister rolled her eyes. "He doesn't want to share a room with a six-year-old, Sonya." Turning to her parents, she said, "Couldn't we buy him a bed and put it in the library room? We could take down our art so he could hang pictures of his family or whatever."

"That's very thoughtful, Taylor," Mrs. Prestwood said.

"Could he walk us to school?" Sonya wanted to know.

My whole body began to tingle as I sat there listening to their conversation. It didn't even seem real. More like a show I was watching on TV.

Mr. and Mrs. Prestwood smiled, and Mr. Prestwood turned to me. "Matt, this is something you'd have to explore with your parents.

188

Obviously. But let me say this. I know how to take a kid with God-given talent like yours and turn him into a real basketball player. By the time you were a senior . . . trust me, college coaches would be beating down your door."

"We're talking about your future," Mrs. Prestwood said. "Do you understand how valuable a free education is these days?"

Early the next morning, Mr. Prestwood drove me back to his high school. He didn't park this time. He handed me a key to the gym and reached over to open my door, saying, "If I pick you up at three, that means you'll be alone in there for almost eight hours. You okay with that?"

I slid out of the car. "Definitely, sir."

He smiled and gave me a little salute before slowly pulling away.

I flipped on the lights as soon as I got inside the gym. I pulled out the rack of leather basketballs and tied my shoes and took out my notebook.

I spent the first hour shooting threes from various spots around the arc and jotting down how many I made out of each hundred. Then I did a series of ballhandling drills. Then I shot free throws. Then I played imaginary games of one-on-one to the point that I was dripping sweat.

If someone peeked their head inside the gym, they'd probably think I was the most dedicated basketball player around. But being alone in a gym was actually really hard for me. Always had been. And as I plopped down on the court to rest, I realized something. Maybe it wasn't the game itself I was so obsessed with, but all the stuff that came with it. When I played ball, I felt a sense of control.

A sense of belonging. And when I played *well*, it gave me a sense of meaning.

When Mr. Prestwood had asked how much time I wanted in the gym, I'd told him, "As much as possible." But I'd only said that because I knew it would impress him. Because I knew it would reinforce the version of me he'd been building inside his head. In reality, I'd barely been in the gym two hours and I was already *bored out of my mind!*

Did all this make me a fraud?

I lay on my back and stared up into the rafters, thinking about the Prestwoods' offer. Thinking about what it would be like to live in a big house on a tree-lined street, so far away from all I knew. Thinking about what it would be like to get great coaching and maybe even play for a championship.

Eventually I found myself flipping through my notebook, reading through all my stats and trying to remember which courts I'd been at when I'd shot my best. But there weren't just shooting stats in my notebook. There were some poems mixed in there, too. Random things I'd written down when I'd been especially lonely. Waiting for the bus outside Muni Gym in Balboa Park. Crossing through the zoo parking lot. Sitting near the edge of the cliff across from Glen Park, looking out over the endless ocean.

I'd never shown my writing to anyone because I didn't think guys *like me* were supposed to write poems. It seemed too sensitive. But as I flipped to a fresh page and started a new one, I had another thought. Writing, I knew, was something I did to express myself, but maybe basketball was, too. Maybe they were more similar than I'd ever imagined.

• • •

I couldn't hear a *thing* when I stepped off the plane in San Diego. My ears were plugged up so bad, it felt like I was underwater.

No one was waving for me when I came down the jet bridge this time, so I took the escalator down to baggage claim. When I didn't see anyone there, either, I exited the airport and stood by the curb, looking all around. I watched a military family reunite and a group of businessmen hurry after the rental car shuttle. I watched a police officer motion for cars to move along.

After a few minutes, I saw something familiar. Our old, beat-up Volkswagen bug.

To my surprise, it was my old man in the driver's seat.

I hustled over to where he'd stopped and tossed my duffel in the back and climbed into the passenger's seat and closed my door. As we pulled away from the curb, he said something I couldn't make out. "What?" I asked, and on a whim I clenched my nose with my thumb and forefinger and blew. To my astonishment, my ears popped, and suddenly I could hear again.

"I said it's good to have you back," he told me.

"Thanks," I said. And then I just sat there, staring through the windshield as we merged onto the highway.

As I studied the cars all around us, speeding up or slowing down, changing lanes, I realized I was never going to do high school away from home. Even if it meant my life might be a little bit smaller here. Or more ordinary. Even if it meant college coaches might never beat down my door. This wasn't just where I belonged, I realized. It was where I wanted to be, too. At least for now.

Neither of us said another word the rest of the way home, but I felt like I could hear everything.

MATT DE LA PEÑA is the Newbery Medal–winning author of *Last Stop on Market Street*. He is also the author of the award-winning picture books *Milo Imagines the World*, *Carmela Full of Wishes*, *Love*, and *A Nation's Hope: The Story of Boxing Legend Joe Louis* and seven critically acclaimed young adult novels. Matt teaches creative writing and visits schools and colleges throughout the country. You can visit Matt at MattdelaPena.com or follow him on Twitter and Instagram @MattdelaPena.

ACKNOWLEDGMENTS

Getting to edit and publish a second book about hope featuring personal experiences by many of my favorite humans is a true honor and privilege; for helping me make it happen, special thanks to the amazing team at Philomel and Penguin Young Readers for all the support. I appreciate you all so much. An extra-special shout-out to my publisher and editor, Jill Santopolo. Thanks for adopting *Hope Wins*. I'm so grateful to have gotten this opportunity to collaborate with you. Cheryl Eissing—you thought you'd gotten away but alas! Once again, your editorial help has been invaluable.

So much appreciation for Vashti Harrison and her gift of the incredible art that adorns *Hope Wins*—I can't imagine anything more perfect for this collection. Thank you for creating the cover of my dreams.

Team Hope: Imagine a blue BELIEVE sign above my ask of you. You walked by and smacked that sign hard. I'll be forever grateful to you for making time to support NTTBF. For many of you, NTTBF is the place where our worlds collided, and your efforts to pay it forward by supporting North Texas readers will not be forgotten. I believe because of each of you.

Susan James, Bryan Crandall, Kim Herzog, and Rebecca Marsick—you are the very best hope dealers out there. Thanks for always championing education, stories, and young people.

Zoom Peeps: On the eve of my birthday in 2020, you joined me virtually to celebrate. Two years later, our weekly get-togethers have been one of my greatest joys. Sarah Mlynowski, Stu Gibbs, Julie Buxbaum, Gordon Korman, James Ponti, Melissa Posten, Max Brallier, Christina Soontornvat, Karina Yan Glaser, and sometimes Elizabeth Eulberg from afar—thank you for providing endless laughter, so many random texts, and all the *Ted Lasso* love and critique I didn't know I needed.

Kiawah Crew: Ally Carter, Carrie Ryan, and Rachel Hawkins—let's never stop finding reasons to run toward beaches and chips and dip.

Cheers to the Down Under Gang, especially Becky Albertalli, Charlotte the Koala, Adele Walsh, and Will Kostakis for reminding me hope is everywhere. Reunion tour ASAP.

Rosebuds: Though this pandemic life has been challenging in so many ways, cherished friends have continued to make all the difference. Special shout-outs to Sid Grant, Kristin Treviño, Angie Mahalik, Milissa Vo, Alicia Montgomery, Jill Bellomy, Amy Toombs, Nicole Caliro, Suzanne Crowley, Libba Bray, Sylvia Vardell, and the LHS Cool Kids Club: Kevin Russ, Ronnie Moore, Cindy Garcia Kreiner, and Monica Roberts. Y'all are the best pals out there!

Sometimes your favorite family is the family you pick for yourself. I'm looking at you, Angie Thomas, Auntie J, and Kobe. Thanks for always giving me a place to go when I run away (besides your warmth and welcome, you know I can't resist chicken and pickles on a stick). My chosen sisters: Nancy Vance, Laticia Porter, Sarah

Burey, Laura Francis, Lisa Bua, April Bedford, Lizette Serrano, Venessa Carson, and Dina Sherman. Y'all are truly some of the best women I know. Thank you for so many years of love and support.

Finally, and most importantly, though my hope is inspired by so many, it's always firmly rooted in the Brocks and Littles, but most especially in my husband, Michael, my precious girls Madeleine and Olivia, Winnie, and the legacy of my beloved mom and the OG hope dealer, Irmgard Klebe Little.